modifying classroom behavior
REVISED

A Manual of Procedure For Classroom Teachers

Nancy K. Buckley
Psychologist, Spanish Peaks Mental Health Center, Pueblo, Colorado

Hill M. Walker
Department of Special Education, University of Oregon, Eugene, Oregon

RESEARCH PRESS COMPANY
2612 NORTH MATTIS AVE.
CHAMPAIGN, ILLINOIS 61820

Illustrations by **Marsha Ludlam-Zimbleman**

Introduction

"What's with schools today?" Nearly everyone on the street has a strong opinion on what our schools should be teaching and how they should be doing that teaching. Much of the focus of concern is currently on the environment in which the child should be taught. Among educators, debates continue over open, informal classrooms versus self-contained classroom units. Meanwhile, legislative mandates are requiring that children be educated in the least restrictive, most "normal" setting possible. This reverses the trend for the last twenty-five years of developing special classrooms for the special needs child. Now the child may be in a special classroom a portion of the day but is "mainstreamed" with his regular classroom peers the majority of the day. While the effects on the children have yet to be systematically proven, we do know about the additional demands this places on the teacher. The teacher is expected to deal with the individual needs of children who have diverse educational backgrounds, motivations, and skills.

While this is a difficult task, it is not impossible. Since it was published in 1970, *Modifying Classroom Behavior* has received tremendous positive response. Teachers find that its techniques provide direction in helping them meet the needs of all children. In this revision, we have kept the basic structure of the text the same. We have, however, added information and classroom examples derived from additional work over the past eight years.

The intent behind the use of behavioral principles has been to develop a science for human interactions and education. Some people fear that using scientific principles will depersonalize education. Our conviction is that only when teachers understand the real impact of the environment upon performance can they begin *to help* each child reach his own potential.

To some, the terms behavior management or behavior control imply the teacher forcing a child into a particular mold. Unfortunately this happens inadvertently in classrooms where teachers have not been taught behavioral principles. When the belief is that children act the way they do because of internal states, it is all too easy to stereotype a child because of his cultural background, his sex, or a handicapping condition. When these stereotypes exist, the teacher unconsciously develops incorrect expectations for that child. These stereotypes also exist for the acting out child. All too often we have entered classrooms to find a child doing no academic work because the teacher has found that he is less antagonistic if left to draw pictures. Teaching a child to "be still, be quiet, and be docile" (Winnett and Winkler, 1972) comes from frustration, *not* from knowing environmental procedures.

It is our hope that all children develop a positive self-concept *and* the ability to learn from their exposure to school. The two are equally important. It is as deplorable to have a child graduate from school at age eighteen who has enjoyed himself but does not know how to read or write well enough to fill out an employment application as it is to have a rigid system where a child has been frightened or ridiculed into learning his multiplication facts. The amount of freedom any individual has is based on the number of options available to him. Most of us would agree that a good education is an important option. For a child to be able to utilize that option, the teacher must be fully aware of how the environment affects the child. *Modifying Classroom Behavior* was written to help the teacher understand these environmental effects and to utilize the techniques within any classroom setting.

N. K. B.
H. M. W.

iv

To the Reader

This book has been written for teacher trainees and practicing teachers. The attempt has been to keep the book as brief and nontechnical in its terminology and concepts as possible without omitting relevant information. For those students and teachers interested in learning more about the procedures and applications of behavior modification, we have included a list of suggested readings (page 129).

In developing the format of the text, the authors chose to incorporate both prose and programmed items to form a semiprogrammed content.* This design was selected to enhance reader interest and at the same time make use of the advantages of programmed instruction. Programmed instruction has been shown effective in learning material because it incorporates: (a) immediate feedback, (b) small steps, (c) active responding, and (d) self-pacing.

The chapters have been divided into sets. Each set represents a different concept important to the chapter focus. Each set begins with a prose section designed to present all new materials.

The programmed items were selected to give feedback to the reader regarding understanding of the prose material. In addition, the programmed items, or frames, incorporate classroom application of the concepts.

It is important that the reader respond actively to each

*Smith, W. I. and Moore, J. W. *Conditioning and instrumental learning.* New York: McGraw-Hill, 1966.

of the items. The response areas are large enough for responses to be written directly into the text. A folded paper should be used to conceal the answers at the bottom of the page. Once a response has been made, the reader moves the paper far enough to check his answer. Learning is much more effective if the reader responds prior to checking the answer. If any questions are not answered correctly, reread the preceding prose section before continuing.

Each of the programmed items requires one of the following responses:

1. Fill in the missing word. "When the reader actually writes the answer down, he is using the principle of active _____ ."

2. Circle the correct response of two choices. "If each step the student takes is small, he (is/is not) likely to make errors."

3. Check the appropriate answer or answers from several possible choices. "Which of the following are principles of programmed instruction?"

   ____ a. Immediate confirmation.
   ____ b. Active responding.
   ____ c. Hidden "trick" questions.
   ____ d. Self-pacing.
   ____ e. Rapid skimming.

Many of the sets contain exhibits. These exhibits are excerpts from actual research done in the field of behavior modification. The exhibits were selected to illustrate and support the

1. responding   2. is not   3. a, b, d

various concepts in the book as well as to serve as stimuli to the reader for further study.

Since the excerpts are in most cases direct quotes from journals, the language is more technical than that of the book. However, complete understanding of the exhibits is not necessary for mastery of the text.

The program has been field tested in classes for regular elementary teachers. The data from these classes were used to revise items.

Contents

Part 1 Basic Principles

Chapter 1　How Behaviors are Learned

SET 1:　Acquisition of Behavior

How *are* behaviors learned? Anyone walking into a classroom sees learning in process. But learning is much more than lectures and workbooks. Every facet of our lives is shaped and molded by the cues and reinforcement of the environment. Tammy learns to be shy, Joyce to be assertive, Joseph to be passive, and Bill to like sports because of the way the environment reacts to their separate behaviors. Even the objects of physiological drives such as the types of food we eat, the people we find attractive and many other behaviors which we take for granted are learned from our associates and society in general.

A child comes to school at five or six years of age with a tremendous background of learning. His environment has "told" him what to expect from school and how to react to it. Once he is in school, his experiences either verify or negate his earlier ideas of school.

We hope that all children come to school feeling confident in their own abilities and in the ability to enjoy and benefit from school experiences. But this is not always the case. Thus four alternatives are possible after a child enters school:

A.　The child feels confident in her own ability, her behaviors match those expected in the classroom, and the reactions of the environment (teachers, peers, etc.) reinforce her behaviors. Thus, the relationship between child and teacher is mutually rewarding.

3

   B.   The child feels confident in his own ability but his behaviors *do not* match with what is expected in the classroom. This can often happen with a child from a different cultural or geographic background. It becomes a matter of the child readjusting his perceptions of appropriate behavior, the teacher adjusting her perceptions, or some intermediate compromise. If this mismatch is handled insensitively, the child comes to see himself as bad or school as bad. In either case, he is likely to feel "turned off" by school.

   C.   The child does not feel confident in her own ability, and *does not* come with the necessary behaviors for classroom performance. If the teacher shares these views and the classroom does not have the extra time to teach the child the necessary skills, the child and his environment tend to reinforce behaviors of failure. Unfortunately, this often happens in special school programs where the child is labeled as "different" and, therefore, not as good as the child who is making it without auxiliary programs.

D. The child is not confident in her own ability but *does* have the necessary behaviors for school performance. Programs geared to building self-confidence and school skills can be important, particularly prior to school enrollment. Thus preschool programs can develop the skills within the child so that she will be able to work to her maximum within the school setting. Then if all classroom teachers recognize that much of each child's academic behavior and most of her social behaviors have been learned, they can work toward maximizing the child's abilities.

Given that a child's behaviors are so closely tied to the environment, we can change our immediate environment and thus change the child's behavior. At the same time, we must be prepared to accept responsibility for misbehaviors that occur during our contacts with the child.

When undesirable behaviors are present we can assume they are a result of (a) the correct (adaptive) behavior never having been learned, or (b) an incorrect (maladaptive) behavior having been learned which conflicts with the performance of the correct behavior. The difference between these two processes has important implications for the treatment strategies employed. For example, before punishing a maladaptive response, a teacher should be aware of whether an alternative adaptive response is in the child's repertoire. If the response is not, it should be taught prior to, or at the same time as, eliminating the maladaptive response.

1. By environment is meant:

   ___ a. the geographical climate in which we live.
   ___ b. the physical surroundings only, such as city vs.
   country.
   ___ c. the surroundings of a person including people,
   institutions and norms.

2. Most of the things we generally consider part of a person's "personality" are (learned/not learned) from the environment.

3. A new child is admitted to the classroom. If he does not raise his hand when responding, we must assume:
   ___ a. he has not learned to raise his hand.
   ___ b. an incorrect behavior, talking out, has been learned.
   ___ c. either a or b, or both.

4. Upon further investigation we find that the child has been ill and tutored at home for three years prior to entering this class. Which of the responses in 3, above, might we assume to be correct?

5. Suppose instead that the child has been going to public school for four years but still shouts out answers. We notice the teacher acknowledges his answers. Which of the choices in 3, above, is correct?

1. c

2. learned

3. c

4. a

5. b

6. At a parent conference you mention to Ricky's mother that he loses his temper frequently. She responds by saying, "I know, but what can I do; he gets that from his father. His side of the family is known for their tempers—they're Irish, you know." From this information you know:

    ___ a. that Ricky has inherited his temper from his parent.
    ___ b. that Ricky may have *learned* to act the way he does from the actions of a parent.

7. The information given by the mother is of little help in solving Ricky's problem. Such statements appear to be attempts at excusing the behavior rather than preventing it. We can assume that Ricky and his father "lose" their tempers not because of inherited traits, but because in the past temper losses have been _____ . Or, Ricky and his father have not learned an appropriate alternative _____ . Or both.

6. b   7. learned; response (behavior)

SET 2:   Reinforcement

We continue to perform certain behaviors over time because we learn it is beneficial to do so. This benefit may be something pleasant—positive reinforcement—or it may be the result of an unpleasant event being taken away—negative reinforcement.

Behaviors, whether adaptive or maladaptive, are learned because of the benefits they produce from the environment (reinforcers). Each time reinforcement occurs immediately following a behavior it becomes more likely that the behavior will be repeated. However, if behaviors are not reinforced (that is, they are ignored or punished) it is likely that they will stop occurring.

EXHIBIT

To illustrate the principle that reinforcement alone can increase a behavior and its withdrawal can decrease that same behavior, researchers often use a "reversal of contingencies" design. With this procedure the behavior under study is measured, an experimental variable is applied (in this case reinforcement) and any change is noted. If a change in behavior occurs (see $Reinf._1$), the experimental variable (reinforcement) is withdrawn or altered (see Reversal). If the change was due to the reinforcement, the measured behavior should be reduced to approximate pre-experimental baseline levels.

In a study by Hall, Lund, and Jackson (1968) the effects of teacher attention on study behavior were measured. With one first-grade and five third-grade children—described as having disruptive or dawdling behavior—the experimenters were able to increase study behavior with teacher attention for study behavior and by ignoring nonstudy behaviors. During a reversal of contingencies, attention was given only after periods of nonstudy behavior. This reversal produced low rates of study behavior.

The following graph represents the study behavior for one subject in the Hall et al. study.

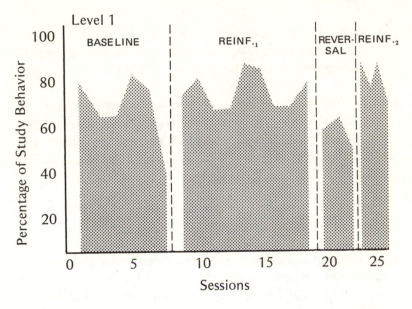

Figure 1 ". . . study occurred in approximately 88% of the intervals of Reinforcement and at no time went below that of the highest baseline rate. A brief reversal produced a marked decrease in study to a mean rate of 60%. However, when reinforcement for study was reinstated, study again rose to above baseline rate." (p. 10)

8. By making a reinforcer available we increase the likelihood that the child will practice what we teach him. A common word for a positive _____ is reward.

8. reinforcer

9. A child who is usually noisy in the hall has been very quiet and asks to carry the balls. Letting him carry the balls can serve as a _____ for walking quietly in the hall.

10. When a child does well on a quiz, he can be praised. Praise serves as a reinforcer for good grades and tends to (increase/decrease) the chances of another good paper.

11. In discussion periods one child waves his hand and impatiently says, "I know, I know," when the teacher poses a question to the class. If the teacher calls on this child, she is reinforcing _____ _____ and _____ _____ .

12. Thus we can expect hand waving and verbal outbursts to (increase/decrease) for this child.

13. A young child learning to read frequently looks at the teacher for approval. When the teacher smiles and indicates the child is reading correctly, we can assume it is desirable or _____ to the child. Thus, the child is more likely to continue attempts at reading.

14. If no one listens to the child read or tells the child he is not reading correctly, the child is not reinforced. In this case the behavior will tend to _____ _____ .

9. reinforcer (or reward)

10. increase

11. hand waving;
    verbal outbursts

12. increase

13. reinforcing (or rewarding)

14. drop out (or stop occurring)

15. Reinforcers effectively shape our lives as adults as well. Think of a time a colleague you respect praised you for a particular task. The chances are good that you worked even harder at the task the next time, whether it was a bulletin board, a math component, etc. The chances are you will spend _____ time doing it and maybe even enjoy it more.

15. more

SET 3: Modeling

It is important to look at how new behaviors are learned, that is, behaviors which have never been displayed before by the child. One method for learning new behaviors is by observation and imitation. A child sees or hears someone perform a particular behavior and he may copy or imitate that behavior. This type of imitative behavior is referred to as *modeling.* We see another person, the model, do something and we copy it. Modeling is most likely to occur when the observer sees the model obtain some type of reinforcer for emitting the behavior. Experimental work (Bandura and Walters, 1963b) gives strong support to acquisition of both adaptive and maladaptive behavior through modeling.

Modeling is very obvious in the behaviors of young children. Most children learn to speak, ride bicycles, identify with their sex, and so forth, by imitating the actions of others.

Throughout life we are guided in our actions by film, verbal, and actual models. The use of a model can be a constructive way to build up desirable behaviors in children. The child is more likely to imitate the model if she likes the model or can identify with that model. This is one reason it is important to have a variety of teaching models available to students.

EXHIBIT

In a study designed to test for delayed imitation of deviant models in the absence of the models, Bandura, Ross, and Ross (1961) "exposed one group of nursery-school children to aggressive adult models and a second group to models who displayed inhibited and nonaggressive behavior. Half of the children in each of these conditions observed models of the same sex as themselves, while the remaining children in each group were exposed to models of the opposite sex. For the aggressive-model group the model exhibited unusual forms of physical and verbal aggression toward a large inflated plastic doll. In contrast, the nonaggressive-model group observed an adult who sat very quietly, totally ignoring the doll and the instruments of aggression that had been placed in the room.

"The children who observed the aggressive models displayed a great number of precisely imitative aggressive responses, whereas such responses rarely occurred in either the nonaggressive-model group or the control group. Moreover, children in the nonaggressive-model group displayed the inhibited behavior characteristic of their model to a greater extent than did the control children. In addition, the results [Bandura, Ross, and Ross, 1963] indicated that film-mediated models are as effective as real-life models in transmitting deviant patterns of behavior." (p. 61)

16. When a teacher says, "Look how nicely Johnny sits in his chair," she is using Johnny as a model for the right way to _____ .

17. A gangster hero on TV may serve as a film _____ for illegal behavior.

18. A well-mannered child who is the subject of a book read in class may be a verbal _____ for good student behavior.

Based on what you have read thus far on reinforcement and modeling, consider the following hypothetical situations (19—22).

19. In Miss Brown's fourth-grade class, Joe throws a pencil at Bob in the front of the room. Miss Brown is busy helping a youngster and does not notice, but many of the children notice and giggle and look at Joe. The likelihood of Bob throwing a pencil is (increased/decreased) after seeing Joe throw one.

20. Miss Brown saw Joe throw the pencil and made him stay in during recess. After observing this interaction, Bob would be (more/less) likely to model Joe's behavior of throwing pencils.

21. After watching Joe throw the pencil, Bob throws a pencil at Joe's desk. Miss Brown sees Bob and sends him to the principal's office. In this case Bob did not receive reinforcement for modeling Joe's behavior. Therefore, the behavior is likely to _____ .

16. sit (in a chair)	18. model	20. less
17. model	19. increased	21. decrease

22. Bob flips a pencil toward Joe which goes unnoticed except by Joe, who giggles and again throws a pencil. If we assume that the attention from Joe is reinforcing, we can expect Bob's throwing to (increase/decrease) in frequency.

23. Miss A, a student teacher in Mr. C's fifth-grade class, has trouble getting the children to quiet down after art class. She notices Mr. C set a 3-minute egg timer and the noise ends abruptly after this period. The reinforcer available to Mr. C in this case is:

____ a. knowing Miss A is having trouble with discipline.
____ b. the egg timer.
____ c. the quiet classroom.

24. If Mr. C is an effective model for Miss A, the next time she wants a quiet classroom she will:

____ a. have Mr. C quiet the classroom.
____ b. use an egg timer.
____ c. eliminate art class.

22. increase   23. c   24. b

SET 4: Shaping

Another method of teaching behaviors or skills, in addition to modeling, is the method of *successive approximations* (shaping) and *chaining.* If a behavior has never been exhibited by a child, we cannot reinforce the behavior. Therefore, to teach some behaviors, we must reward behaviors which are close to, or approximate, the desired behaviors.

As the general response comes to be exhibited more frequently, we reward a step closer to the desired specific response. From this gradual refining of the reinforced response we get the name successive approximation.

An example of the method of successive approximation, or shaping, is the gradual progression in teaching a child to print. At first any approximation of the letter is accepted— for example, *N* for the letter "N." Gradually the child is required to make strokes more closely like an "N" before the teacher says "good." Reinforcing each small step toward a better "N" is using the method of successive approximation.

Not only must a child be taught how to make an "N" of the right shape, but also the proper size and placement on a page. Putting all of these responses together to make one complete response is called chaining.

EXHIBIT

The following study illustrates not only the shaping procedure but also how aware the teacher must be of the contingencies operating when attempting to alter deviant behavior. Wolf, Risley, and Mees (1964), in a now classical study, used shaping to get a three-year-old autistic boy to wear glasses.

"During the first several sessions a conditioned reinforcer was established by having the clicks of a toy noisemaker followed by Dicky's receiving small bites of candy or fruit. The click soon became a discriminative stimulus, and after each click Dicky would go to the bowl where the reinforcers were placed.

"Since Dicky had worn the prescription glasses for

a few seconds on at least one occasion and had not left them on, it was assumed that wearing them was not immediately reinforcing. The glasses might even have been mildly aversive since they would drastically change all visual stimuli, as well as force the eyes into greater accommodation. Also, glasses with the full prescription had been paired in the past with attempts to physically force glasses-wearing.

"For these reasons we decided not to begin with the actual prescription glasses. Instead, several empty glasses frames were placed around the room and Dicky was reinforced for picking them up, holding them, and carrying them about. Slowly, by successive approximations, he was reinforced for bringing the frames closer to his eyes.

"The original plan was, after he was wearing the lenseless frames, to introduce plain glass and then prescription lenses in three steps of progressing severity. This was not the actual sequence of events, however, since our shaper met with considerable difficulty in getting Dicky to wear the glassless frames in the proper manner, i.e., with the ear pieces over instead of under the ears and the eye openings in line with the eyes. Furthermore, it was impossible to help place the frames correctly since Dicky became upset when anyone touched any part of his head.

"The slow progress was probably attributable to two factors. First, the attendant, although co-operative, was inexperienced and imprecise with the shaping procedure. Secondly, due to the reluctance of the ward staff to deprive the child of food we began with reinforcers such as candy and fruit. It soon became obvious, however, that, at least for this child, these were rather weak reinforcers.

"After the first two weeks we attempted to increase deprivational control by using breakfast as a shaping session, bites of breakfast now being dependent upon approximations to the wearing of glasses. Two weeks later we added to the glasses larger adult ear pieces and a 'roll bar' which would go over the top of his head and guide the ear pieces up and over the ears.

"After wearing the glasses was established in these sessions, it could be maintained with other, less manipulable reinforcers. For example, the attendant would tell Dicky, 'Put your glasses on and let's go for a walk.' Dicky was usually required to wear the glasses during meals, snacks, automobile rides, walks, outdoor play, etc. If he removed the glasses, the activity was terminated.

"At the time of Dicky's release from the hospital he had worn the glasses for more than 600 hours and was wearing them about 12 hours a day." (pp. 309 - 310)

25. In using the methods of successive approximation and chaining to get a shy child to speak in front of the room, which of the following techniques would be used:

_____ a. require the child to give a three-minute report each day on various topics of interest.

_____ b. begin at a level he can tolerate. For example, reading in seat, reading to small group standing beside desk, reading to teacher only, reading in isolation, etc. After he feels comfortable at this step, gradually progress to the next logical step— moving closer to the front of the room, increasing the audience size, etc.

_____ c. concentrate on his strengths. Work on encouraging the child to do the things he does well and don't require him to talk in front of the room.

25. b

26. In a gym class several of the boys cannot chin themselves for fifteen seconds to pass the physical fitness test. Therefore, Mr. B records the level which they can achieve—holding on to bar, pulling self halfway up, maintaining correct posture one second, etc. Over time he gradually *increases* the amount expected for each boy. He keeps an accurate record so as not to pass the child's physical limitations but at the same time to continually increase the achievement level by small amounts. This is an example of the method of _____ _____ .

27. There are a variety of ways to correct "out-of-seat behavior" in a child who has trouble remaining in his seat. One of the most positive approaches for both teacher and child is to use successive approximations. Mrs. T has recorded that Ron seldom stays in his seat for longer than five minutes at a time. Her goal is to get him to stay in his seat fifteen minutes at a time without getting up, which is what most of her third-grade pupils average. Her first step should be to:

___ a. reinforce him each time he returns to his desk.
___ b. wait until he has been in his chair four to five minutes. Go to his desk and praise him or give a token reinforcer.
___ c. tell him that other children can sit for fifteen minutes and if he sits in his chair for fifteen minutes he will get a point.
___ d. remind him each time he is out of his seat that he should sit quietly in order to get points.

26. successive approximation   27. b (A shorter time period might be necessary for another student but the teacher must be careful not to reinforce the act of getting out of his seat.)

28. When Ron has been able to sit for several five-minute periods, this is a sign to Mrs. T to:

_____ a. increase the time required to ten minutes.
_____ b. increase the time required to fifteen minutes (her goal).
_____ c. increase the time required to six to seven minutes.

29. Assume that Mrs. T increases the time required for in-seat behavior to seven minutes. Ron sits approximately five and one-half minutes, then leaves his seat. This occurs several times in succession; each time he fails to stay for the full seven minutes. This is a clue that the step was too _____ and she should drop back to five and one-half minutes until he consistently succeeds at that level. She should then continue gradually increasing the time requirement until he can sit for fifteen minutes at a time. (See intermittent reinforcement for maintenance, page 39.)

30. A child has just moved to a new open classroom school. His previous schooling has been at a very structured school. His past academic records are good but he now wanders from group to group and fails to complete assignments. The teacher should:

_____ a. talk to him about what is bothering him so he can't settle down to work.
_____ b. keep him after school to complete assignments.
_____ c. give him considerable structure initially in terms of desk arrangement, length of assignments, etc., and gradually reduce the amount of structure.
_____ d. ignore the wandering since he will settle down when he is ready.

28. c   29. large   30. c

SUMMARY
1. The behaviors people exhibit are due to the interchange between the environment and the person.
2. Adaptive behaviors and maladaptive behaviors are learned in the same way.
3. Behaviors which are rewarded tend to be repeated.
4. New behaviors can be learned through one of two methods:
   a. modeling of someone or something in the environment.
   b. shaping and chaining of small responses to more closely approximate larger behaviors.

Chapter 2 **Why Behaviors Continue To Be Performed (Maintained)**

SET 1: Reasons for Studying Maintenance

When presented with a behavior problem, it often appears that the reason a child exhibits a certain behavior is because of some *one* thing that occurred in his past. As the following example illustrates, this can often be misleading.

Betty, age five, throws tantrums when separated from her mother. The mother recalls that the first time she was aware of the behavior was after a long hospitalization when Betty was three. From this information we might quickly assume that Betty's temper tantrums at age five are caused by a traumatic separation earlier in her life. However, the child psychologist working with Betty's mother also discovers that each time Betty becomes upset her mother agrees not to leave, thus reinforcing the tantrums by giving Betty her way.

This example illustrates two important reasons for not looking for some original *cause:*

1. Determining how or why a child first performed a behavior is nearly impossible. We, of course, cannot directly observe the past history of an individual. Therefore, we must rely on reports from other persons or the individual himself. This type of reporting can be grossly inaccurate. In this case, we cannot be sure Betty had never had temper tantrums before the hospital separation.

2. The stimulus that maintains the behavior can be very different from the original stimulus for emitting the behavior.

In the illustration, the hospital separation is not causing the tantrums now; rather, the reinforcement from mother remaining home strengthens and maintains the behavior.

It is helpful to look at a situation in terms of (a) the event which occurred prior to the child's response (*the stimulus*); (b) the child's behavior (*the response*); and (c) what followed immediately after the child emitted the behavior (*the consequence*). The stimulus and the consequence are both changes in the child's environment. The response is a single instance of an observable and definable part of a child's behavior.

It is easier to see the relationship between a response and its consequence (a behavioral contingency) by charting the relationship schematically. One notational system which serves this purpose was developed by Mechner (1959). Basically, the schema shows the stimulus situation (S or S_1), the response (R) and the consequence (usually called S_2). A subscript number can be used to show a change in the situation or response, that is, $S_1, S_2 \ldots S_n$ or $R_1, R_2 \ldots R_n$. Thus the basic diagram would be:

$$\left[\begin{array}{l} S_1 \\ R \longrightarrow S_2 \end{array} \right.$$

When using actual situations, it is easier to simply write the event in subscript parentheses. Thus the contingency of leaving for lunch break might be diagrammed as follows:

$$\left[\begin{array}{l} S \;_{\text{(Bell rings)}} \\ R \;_{\substack{\text{(T. excuses} \\ \text{class)}}} \longrightarrow S \;_{\substack{\text{(children leave} \\ \text{room)}}} \end{array} \right.$$

The bracket around the S_1 and R indicates that they occur simultaneously. That is, the situation must be present for the response to occur. The arrow indicates "leads to" or "produces."

In the case of Betty's tantrums, the analysis might be as follows:

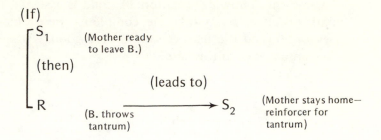

(If)

S_1 (Mother ready to leave B.)

(then)

(leads to)

R $\longrightarrow$ S_2 (Mother stays home— reinforcer for tantrum)

(B. throws tantrum)

1. As a classroom teacher you have a child who vomits when punished or forced to stay after school. You check his medical record and find no physiological reason for the vomiting. Upon calling his mother you learn that he does this frequently at home when punished, but the mother does not know what to do. You should:

    ____ a. refer the child to a psychiatrist.
    ____ b. work with the parents to determine how the vomiting started.
    ____ c. look at your own behavior to see what *you* do when he vomits.

2. Brian, a fourth grader, has a "history" of fighting in the playground. This fighting has continued in the fourth grade. His teacher should:

    ____ a. talk to his previous teachers to determine why he began to fight.
    ____ b. refer him to the school counselor for group therapy.
    ____ c. not allow him on the playground again.
    ____ d. try to determine what is maintaining the behavior (the reinforcer) and eliminate it or change its reinforcing value.

1. c   2. d

3. Assume the following situation: A child is assigned ten math problems (stimulus). He completes the problems (response), and the teacher says, "Very good." What is the consequence in this case?

$$\begin{bmatrix} S & \text{(Assignment)} \\ R & \text{(Working problems)} \end{bmatrix} \longrightarrow S^{R+} \qquad a(?)$$

a. _____

4. A child is turned around talking to a peer. The teacher asks him to face the front of the room. He refuses and so is sent from the room. What are the missing parts of the contingency?

$$\begin{bmatrix} S_1 & \text{(T. "Turn around")} \\ R & (\text{ a (?) }) \end{bmatrix} \longrightarrow S_2 \qquad (\text{ b (?) })$$

a. _____

b. _____

3. a. Teacher praise   4. a. Refusal
    ("Very good")   b. Sent from room

5. Brian is a large boy for his age but does poorly in P.E. activities. The teacher has tried to encourage him to participate but within the first five minutes he trips, pushes, or in some other way upsets another student. When this occurs the teacher sends him off to play by himself.

Identify the contingencies that maintain this behavior.

$$\begin{bmatrix} S_1 & (\ a \ (?) \ ) \\ R & (\ b \ (?) \ ) \end{bmatrix} \longrightarrow S_2 \quad (\ c \ (?) \ )$$

a. _____

b. _____

c. _____

5. a. P.E. period
    b. upsets peers
    c. removal of Brian
       (escape from P.E.)

SET 2: Effects of the Environment

The response is each child's unique way of reacting to the environment. We can't force a change in that response even when the response is detrimental to the child. However, we can change the environment both *before* (Situation 1) the child is expected to perform a response and *after* (Situation 2) he has done something. Changing the environment will make it more (or less, depending on the technique) likely that the behavior will occur again.

There are a variety of ways that the stimulus (Situation 1) can be changed, including:

A.   Instructions—clear, short rules presented orally and in writing.

B.   Verbal preparation to increase motivation—suggesting suspense, novelty, a challenge, or build-up of confidence.

C.   Tools used by child—visual, auditory, or tactile aids.

D.   Clear signals of when the behavior is expected.

6. Often there are one or two children in class who ask to have the instructions and page number repeated for an assignment. The situation can be changed in a variety of ways to prevent this. Which of the following stimulus changes will accomplish this?

_____ a. keeping the instructions concise.
_____ b. increasing the motivation by challenging the students to remember the number.
_____ c. presenting the page number both orally and in writing on the board.
_____ d. waiting until all children are attending and giving a signal indicating the page number is next.
_____ e. lecturing those who aren't attentive.

7. Even behaviors such as stealing and lying can be reduced by carefully structuring *positive* expectations _____ the behavior occurs.

8. The placement of desks and chairs greatly determines the kind of behaviors expected. Placing chairs in a circle before class begins encourages _____ .

9. Signals can also be used to indicate when a response is needed. The hand signals of a conductor all ensure attentiveness and responses at appropriate times. Since active responding assists learning, this method _____ the likelihood of learning while maintaining on-task behavior.

6. a, b, c, d

7. before

8. discussion (talking)

9. increases

10. Research indicates that misbehavior often follows from a child not being able to receive teacher help when he needs it, or feels he needs it. To eliminate this problem, at least two effective systems have been used in the classroom. One system is for each child to have a small tag (attached to his desk or inside his desk) that can be placed on top of the desk to signal the need for help. Thus, the child has his hands free to continue working and, by prior agreement, the teacher will go first to those children who are working.

A second system involves a series of numbers at the teacher's desk such as found in many department store catalogue departments. The first child waiting for help takes Number 1, the second child Number 2 and so on; they then return to their seats to work. As the teacher finishes helping one child she calls out the next number.

Both of these techniques are examples of changing the _____ to bring about a change in child behavior.

10. environment

SET 3: Positive Reinforcement

In understanding why behaviors continue to be performed we can apply the general principle of reinforcement from Chapter 1. When a person (child or teacher) receives a benefit for exhibiting a certain behavior, that behavior is strengthened and will more likely be exhibited again in the future.

Positive reinforcement has an important function in learning new behaviors. It is equally important in maintaining behaviors that are already in a person's repertoire.

Each day we receive reinforcement in a variety of ways for our behavior. Three broad classes of reinforcers available are (1) social reinforcers, (2) token or tangible reinforcers, and (3) intrinsic reinforcers.

By definition a reinforcer is an event which *changes* behavior. Therefore, any of the following may or may not be a reinforcer for any given person. They are only potential reinforcers.

Social Positive Reinforcement

As the term implies, social reinforcers are those that come from other people in our environment. We generally think of praise, agreement, and gestures of affection or approval as reinforcing. In the classroom a word or gesture of approval immediately following a behavior (if reinforcing) strengthens that behavior.

EXHIBIT

"Becker, Madsen, Arnold and Thomas (1967) worked in public schools with teachers who had problem children in their classes. Behaviors exhibited by the students were observed and the frequency of these behaviors was estimated for each child. Each teacher was taught to use praise, smiles, etc., to reinforce good behavior. The rate of appropriate classroom behaviors increased in most cases as soon as teacher approval and recognition were made contingent on such behavior." (Thomas, Becker, and Armstrong, 1968, p. 35).

An extension of this study (Thomas, Becker, and Armstrong, 1968) used a class of 28 elementary students rated by the teacher as "good" . . . "with an above-average distribution of ability and no 'bad' kids." Recordings were made on both teacher and child behaviors.

"The results demonstrated that approving teacher response served a positive reinforcing function in maintaining appropriate classroom behaviors. Disruptive behaviors increased each time approving teacher behavior was withdrawn. When the teacher's disapproving behaviors were tripled, increases appeared most markedly in the gross motor and noise-making categories of disruptive behavior. The findings emphasize again the important role of the teacher in producing, maintaining, and eliminating disruptive as well as pro-social classroom behavior." (p. 35)

Positive Reinforcement With Tokens

A wide variety of token and tangible reinforcers are available in our lives—money, food, promotions, awards, certificates, etc. All of these reinforcers are used to strengthen behaviors considered desirable to the employer or to society. Some reinforcers are originally neutral but acquire their potency from being paired with other reinforcers. These reinforcers are termed acquired or conditioned reinforcers. Money is a conditioned reinforcer because it is valuable not for its own properties but for what it can buy in primary reinforcers.

Many positive rewards can be utilized in the classroom. Tokens are an efficient system for measuring the child's progress toward a backup reward. The token system allows for accumulation of symbols of achievement. These symbols can be poker chips, check marks, stamps, colored papers, stars, etc.

Once a predetermined number of tokens has been earned, the child can trade for a backup reward. Commonly used rewards include candies, films, toys, trips, games, parties, free time and special privileges. A teacher has a variety of activities available within the classroom. Only in cases where the behaviors are excessive and have existed for some period of time should rewards be considered that are elaborate or cost money.

EXHIBIT
"The central aspect of a token system is the pairing of teacher praise with tokens which are backed up by an effective reinforcer. In most effective studies, however, many other procedures have also been used. For example, praise for appropriate behavior and ignoring of disruptive behavior are used at times when tokens are not being dispensed. Time Out (or isolation) is often used when intensely disruptive behaviors occur. Systematic contingencies in the form of privileges are often applied throughout the day. The children following the rules are the ones who get to help teacher, to be first in line, to choose an activity, etc. The principle of shaping is also systematically applied. Praise, privileges, and tokens are not administered for achieving an absolute standard of performance, but for improving behavior or for maintaining a high level of acceptable behavior." (Kuypers, Becker, and O'Leary, 1968, p. 108)

"A token system is not a magical procedure to be applied in a mechanical way. It is simply one tool within a larger set of tools available to the teacher concerned with improving the behavior of children. The full set of equipment is needed to do the job right." (p. 101)

Intrinsic Positive Reinforcement
Intrinsic reinforcers are those available from performing the activity itself. In schools, for example, we assume that the intrinsic reinforcers of satisfaction from knowing, curiosity, novelty and pride in achievement are all operating. It would be difficult, if not impossible, to measure the power of these

intrinsic reinforcers for any one child. However, we can assume the intrinsic value of a reinforcer is low if the child does not continue to perform the behavior.

If the assignments in a classroom are set up properly, they can easily become reinforcing for *all* children. Performing a task for the intrinsic reinforcement available has been observed in infants as young as three months (Piaget, 1929).

Observe any child under three and you will see the absolute delight they experience at being able to perform a task, no matter how imperfect. However, as a child gets older self-doubt, fears of failure, and hesitancy over the difficulty of tasks cause a child to hold back. This is true to some degree for all children. Therefore, in order to help the child overcome his hesitancy to perform, it is often necessary to provide external "proof," in the form of praise or tokens, for performing a task. The extrinsic reinforcers can be an important first step in strengthening intrinsic reinforcers. Once the behavior is being strongly emitted, the contrived or external reinforcers generally can be, and should be, eliminated.

11. Positive reinforcement serves the two functions of:

    a. _____ of new behavior.
    b. _____ of behaviors already exhibited.

12. Each time the child misbehaves he is sent to the principal's office. The number of misbehaviors stays at a high rate with this contingency in operation. We might, therefore, assume that going to the principal's office is

    _____ .

11. a. acquisition,
        learning
     b. maintenance

12. reinforcing (or
        not aversive)

13. Learning to write in school so that one can write letters to friends is an example of (extrinsic/intrinsic) reinforcement.

14. The following reinforcers can be classified as social, token, or intrinsic. Pair each one with the appropriate type of reinforcer.

   a. social   b. token or tangible   c. intrinsic

   ___(1) praise   ___(5) curiosity
   ___(2) ice cream   ___(6) money
   ___(3) feeling of power ___(7) gold stars
   ___(4) attention from   ___(8) toys
        another person   ___(9) success

13. intrinsic

14. (1) a   (4) a   (7) b
    (2) b   (5) c   (8) b
    (3) c   (6) b   (9) c

SET 4: Negative Reinforcement

Negative reinforcement involves the removal of an undesirable or painful stimulus. This removal of the aversive stimulus serves to strengthen the behavior which removes it.

We generally think of shock, physical pain, and loud noises as aversive. In addition, social interactions such as nagging, scolding, embarrassing, and criticizing are generally aversive. For some children with a prior history of pairing aversive events with a person or setting, even the presence of that person or setting can be aversive.

This is what typically happens with an underachieving child. Academic activities become painful when the child has to struggle for answers. Therefore, the child can develop elaborate and varied techniques for "turning off" such aversive events as oral reading and teacher attention.

Typical techniques which underachieving children use—often with tremendous success—include saying "I can't," ignoring teacher initiation, frequent trips to the bathroom and drinking fountain, acting out, and in some cases behaviors such as frequent yawning. (Gaasholt, 1969)

15. Presenting a reinforcer following a desirable behavior is called _____ reinforcement. The termination of an undesirable or aversive event is called _____ reinforcement.

16. Any behavior that terminates the negative reinforcer will tend to be strengthened and occur again. When a child is teased, he hits the teasing classmate. If the teasing stops, there is a good chance that hitting behavior has been (weakened/strengthened).

17. If a sign or comment from the teacher quiets a noisy classroom, then use of the signal is strengthened or maintained because it terminates the negative reinforcer which in this case is the _____ .

18. A child wants very badly to be called upon in recitation. So he waves his hand frantically in the air and hops up and down in his chair. To quiet him down, the teacher calls on him. This removes the negative reinforcer, _____ _____ , for the teacher. Thus one would expect her to (increase/decrease) responding to hand waving.

15. positive;
    negative

16. strengthened

17. noisy classroom (or noise)

18. hand waving;
    increase

19. In 18 the teacher is negatively reinforced for calling on the child. What is the effect of her response on the child? His hand waving was _____ and, therefore, will (increase/decrease).

19. reinforced;
    increase

SET 5: Schedules of Reinforcement

One of the most important rules in successful behavior change is to reinforce the behavior *immediately* after it occurs. The child in the classroom should be praised (or punished) within seconds after the behavior occurs.

In building or strengthening a behavior, how often reinforcement occurs is also important. Reinforcement which follows each time the behavior or response occurs is called continuous reinforcement.

In general, continuous reinforcement results in learning that behavior more rapidly. Therefore, if a teacher wants to teach a child a certain behavior, she should acknowledge it each time it occurs.

Continuous reinforcement is important in the early stages of behavior acquisition. Once the behavior is well established, however, it is better to reinforce only intermittently.

To systematically reinforce a child, it is most effective to set up a schedule of reinforcement. To do this, one decides whether to reinforce the child after a certain period of time (interval schedule) or after a certain number of responses have occurred (ratio schedule). For example, the schedule might specify "reinforce every hour" or it might specify "reinforce every fifth response."

In general, an interval schedule maintains consistent behavior over a longer period of time, but ratio schedules produce higher rates of responding.

20. Sharon is a large, boisterous child who enters the room loudly stomping and yelling each morning. This morning she came in quietly and sat down to read a book. She should be praised within _____ of when she sits down.

20. seconds

21. Ray is a new child in the classroom. Several times the teacher has encouraged him to respond orally with the group, but he hides his face and doesn't speak. In a science recitation period he suddenly raises his hand to respond to a question. As the teacher you see your chance to reinforce him by calling on him. He responds—but with the wrong answer. You should:

_____ a. praise him after class when the other children have gone.

_____ b. find something about his response to praise honestly at that moment.

_____ c. ignore the comment so it won't draw the others' attention.

21. b

22. If a child blurts out comments without raising his hand, he can be taught to raise his hand by reinforcing him each time he _____ _____ _____ .

23. Continuous reinforcement is important in the early stages when the behavior is being _____ . Once the behavior is well established, however, it is better if the reinforcement is intermittent and not _____ .

24. When the subject must perform the same behavior several times for reinforcement, the reinforcement schedule is _____ . That is, reinforcement does not follow each time the behavior occurs.

25. Once the child raises his hand consistently to respond, he need be praised only periodically for the _____ to maintain.

26. Miss A teaches fourth grade. A boy in her class has trouble staying in his seat and working. He walks around the room, talks to his neighbors, looks at the encyclopedias, etc., when the rest of the class is working. Miss A decides to increase staying-in-seat behavior by praising him and giving attention when he is in his seat working. Since she has a large class to teach she, of course, cannot be with him each time he is working. Therefore, she decides that every twenty minutes she will check his behavior and, if he is working, she will praise him. She is reinforcing the boy only after:

___ a. a certain time interval.
___ b. the behavior has occurred X number of times.

22. raises his hand

23. learned (taught or acquired); continuous

24. intermittent

25. behavior (or response)

26. a

27. Miss G has a girl in her sixth-grade class who seldom gets her assignments completed to hand in. Miss G decides to make a chart and to give the girl a star each time she hands in a completed assignment, regardless of the amount of time it takes. The schedule of reinforcement Miss G used is:

—— a. interval schedule.
—— b. ratio schedule.

27. b

SUMMARY

1. For maladaptive behavior already present it is more important to look at why the behavior is being maintained—what is happening now—than why it occurred in the first place. Remember, in the classroom the behavior may be maintained by the response of the teacher or the other students.
2. Social and token reinforcers are important tools for the teacher in controlling classroom behavior.
3. Removing an aversive stimulus (negative reinforcement) is also important in the classroom.
4. To be effective, reinforcement should follow immediately after the response.
5. When teaching a behavior, it should be rewarded each time it occurs. Once the behavior occurs frequently, it should be reinforced only intermittently.

Chapter 3 How Behaviors Can Be Eliminated

It is important to remember that a key element in changing behavior relates to changing what happens immediately following a behavior.

    A.   When the behavior is followed immediately by reinforcement, the likelihood of that behavior occurring again is *strengthened*.

    B.   If a behavior is no longer reinforced, that behavior is likely to become *weaker*.

SET 1:   Punishment

The use of aversive consequences in eliminating behavior has involved considerable controversy, particularly in light of research evidence from some controlled experiments (Estes, 1944; Parke, 1969; Johnston, 1972). In considering the use of punishment, we must keep in mind the goals of education for each individual child. Quieting a disruptive child may be of paramount importance so that the rest of the class can learn. We must, however, consider the effects of punishment on the particular child as well. Often what we consider as punishment only temporarily reduces the behavior but may have serious consequences for that child's feelings about himself and school.

45

Problem children often act the way they do because they do not accept responsibility for their actions. Either they learn to avoid responsibility by talking adults out of imposing consequences for breaking rules, or they convincingly deny breaking the rules. Often the most effective "therapy" is to help a child see his impact on the environment. What he or she does, matters. Therefore, consequences are enforced for both acceptable and unacceptable behaviors. Certainly a child can have input into what are reasonable classroom rules. Once the rules are established, we owe it to the child to enforce the rules with prearranged consequences.

The question becomes: What is effective in reducing behavior? A problem occurs when responses designed to punish deviant behavior do not effectively reduce its frequency and may in some cases accelerate it.

Why do teachers and parents continue to use these techniques if they do not decelerate the behavior? Studies have shown that there is often a suppression of the child's behavior at the time of punishment which leads the teacher to believe what he did or said "worked." And, when the behavior returns later at a higher intensity, we often "blame" it on the child rather than on our own behavior.

How often have you heard, "I must tell Brian five times a day to stay in his seat, yet the minute my back is turned helping another child he is out of his seat again"? Such occurrences are good clues that the technique is not effective.

What we often speak of as punishment involves physical or verbal reprimand for performing a certain behavior. The significant feature of this "punishment" is that it is *socially* administered rather than a natural contingency of the rules. This punishment (spanking, scolding, etc.) often is administered in anger accompanied by a verbal barrage from the one administering the "punishment."

While "punishment" is often the most frequent type of behavior control used, it has several undesirable side effects:

a. When punished, the child may strike back at the

46

object or a socially irrelevant object (for example, he may throw a book).

b.   The teacher (and school) may come to be identified as aversive to the child, especially if punishment is meted out in an angry, threatening tone.

c.   The effects of punishment have been shown to last for a short time. This is due in part to the inconsistency of "punishment" (depending often on the mood of the teacher).

d.   The punished behavior may be suppressed only in the presence of the punishing agent.

The important features to remember in effecting behavior change through punishment are:

a.   Specify the rules to the child before the situation occurs, for example, "The rule at our school is 'no fighting'; anyone found fighting will be sent home for the day."

b.   Do not warn or threaten but carry through with the consequence the *first time* and *every time* the deviant behavior occurs.

c.   Make the consequence (going home) occur immediately following the deviant behavior (fighting).

d.   Make sure the consequence is aversive enough that the child chooses to stop performing the behavior rather than risk receiving the consequences; for example, if a child fights so that he can be sent home, this *is not aversive* and another technique should be used.

e.   Keep the rule infraction in perspective so that the child can be dealt with in a manner that does not insult either the child's or the adult's dignity and self-respect. At the moment the infraction occurs the child's self-respect is obviously not uppermost in our thoughts. However, if humiliated or "backed into a corner," a child will retaliate either at the time or in indirect ways later. Unfortunately, this often seems to confirm how "bad" the child is. Actually, it is a very predictable response considering the attack that the child has received.

47

f.   Make positive reinforcers available for appropriate behaviors. Teaching behaviors through punishment can be seen as trial and error learning. The child is experimenting with how to react to his environment. Each time he tries a behavior he is told through punishment that he has picked a "wrong" choice. To keep the child "motivated" toward trying in school, we must also give recognition for attempts at acceptable behavior.

EXHIBIT

"If punishment is used, it should be used effectively . . . . The humane teacher often resorts to warning the student, 'If you do that again, I will have to punish you.' As a conditioned aversive stimulus, a warning is a mild punishment, but it is also a discriminative stimulus, and a student who is punished only after being warned will discriminate between occasions when behavior is and is not punished and will show the effects of punishment only after a warning has been given." (Skinner, 1968, p. 188)

"What appears to be punishment is sometimes reinforcing; a student misbehaves to annoy his teacher or to be admired by his peers when he takes punishment." (Skinner, p. 190)

". . . a low grade on a paper in composition is part of unprogrammed terminal contingencies which do not respect details of the student's behavior and hence do not teach good writing, but a series of small punishments for bad grammar, illogical construction, and solecisms, for example, may be useful." (Skinner, p.187)

"A fatal principle is 'letting well enough alone'— giving no attention to a student so long as he behaves well and turning to him only when he begins to cause trouble. Under most circumstances, dismissing a class may be reinforcing to the student, but the teacher is likely to dismiss the class when trouble is brewing

and thus reinforce early stages of troublemaking."
(Skinner, p. 190)

1. A child has been told that his paper is unacceptable and that he will have to rewrite it before handing it in. As he returns to his desk he kicks the wastebasket which spills. From what you have learned about punishment, is this a likely behavior? (yes, no)

2. At the beginning of school in the fall you get a boy who refuses to work and, when you attempt to help him or reason with him, he gives back "smart talk." Which one of the following *might* account for his behavior:

____ a. he is like his older brother.
____ b. teachers may have become aversive to him because of his history of punishment.
____ c. he rejects the school experience; doesn't find it meaningful.
____ d. he is hyperactive.

3. A rule has been in effect for two weeks that any child who does not complete his work will have to finish it during recess. The rule has been very effective in increasing the production rate of all the students except Jill. She has missed five recess periods due to incomplete work. Which of the following may contribute to her noncompliance? (may check more than one)

____ a. she has a low metabolism.
____ b. the reinforcer (recess) isn't strong enough.
____ c. the punishment (lack of recess) isn't strong enough.
____ d. she likes to cause trouble.

1. yes   2. b   3. b, c

4. One of the goals of education is to develop children with good independent study skills. Mr. James, the principal, is concerned because Miss E's classroom behaves well in her presence yet becomes disruptive when she leaves the room. What can be assumed about her control procedures?

　　____ a. nothing. All children act up when the teacher is out of the room.
　　____ b. her classroom is too permissive.
　　____ c. she uses aversive control measures when in the classroom.
　　____ d. she is inconsistent in her use of rewards and punishment.

5. Which one of the following forms of punishment would *not* be effective in eliminating the behavior:

　　____ a. a child tries to walk on the teeter-totter, falls and hurts himself.
　　____ b. the class is told that one rule is not to walk on teeter-totters, and that anyone found walking on a teeter-totter will lose one recess. The teacher, upon finding the boy walking on the teeter-totter, mentions without anger that at the next recess he will be unable to go out.
　　____ c. the child walks on the teeter-totter. Upon seeing this, the teacher shakes him and pulls him along to the side of the building where she stands lecturing him.

4. c

5. c

SET 2: Extinction

A behavior that is never reinforced will decrease in strength and may eventually disappear. The process of purposefully withholding reinforcement, which has previously been given following a behavior, is called extinction.

The reduction in behavior does not happen immediately, however. When the behavior is no longer followed by a reinforcer, the child (or adult) will generally try even harder for a time to produce the reinforcer. It is important to remember: When attempting to eliminate or reduce a behavior through extinction, the behavior may temporarily increase after the start of extinction. If the child gets attention at that point, we have taught him to use even more extreme measures to get attention. If attention is the goal, even critical comments by the teacher can be rewarding. It follows that there are some behaviors that should not be ignored because we cannot allow them to increase initially in the classroom. Ignoring would be inappropriate for behaviors that would be dangerous to the child or someone else, that would serve as bad models for the rest of the class, or when there is a danger that the behavior would be rewarded at a higher level.

How rapidly the behavior is extinguished (decreased) depends on the past reinforcement history of the child. If the child has been intermittently reinforced (see Chapter 2) for a long period of time, it will take a long time to extinguish the behavior. Since most learned behaviors in our environment have been maintained by inconsistent, and thus intermittent, reinforcement, it takes patience and consistent nonreinforcement of the behavior to eliminate it from a classroom by extinction.

EXHIBIT

Zimmerman and Zimmerman (1966) reported the use of extinction with an eleven-year-old boy of normal intelligence. The boy "displayed temper tantrums (kicking, screaming, etc.), spoke baby talk, and incessantly made irrelevant comments or posed irrelevant questions."

Observing a temper tantrum prior to entering the class, "*E* asked the attendant to put the boy in the classroom at his desk and to leave the room. Then *E* closed the door. The boy sat at his desk, kicking and screaming; *E* proceeded to her desk and worked there, ignoring [the child]. After two or three minutes, the boy, crying softly, looked up at *E*. Then *E* announced that she would be ready to work with him as soon as he indicated that he was ready to work. He continued to cry and scream with diminishing loudness for the next four or five minutes. Finally, he lifted his head and stated that he was ready. Immediately, *E* looked up at him, smiled, went to his desk, and said, 'Good, now let's get to work.' The boy worked quietly and cooperatively with *E* for the remainder of the class period."

"After several weeks [repeating this procedure with each tantrum], class tantrums disappeared entirely." (p. 95)

6. If a child is aware that he is making a noise in the classroom by loudly tapping his pencil and the noise goes unnoticed—peers as well as teacher ignore the behavior—it will probably _____ .

6. decrease, stop, terminate

7. In the example of the pencil tapping child, if the teacher uses the process of extinction, she no longer acknowledges his behavior as disruptive and she has told the other children not to turn around and pay attention. Thus the child's reward for pencil tapping has been cut off and he may tap even louder to get the attention. It is important that the teacher not acknowledge the tapping regardless of the loudness because any acknowledgment will _____ the new intensity.

8. The process of _____ also works on desirable behaviors. A child comes in each morning and sits in his chair quietly ready for work while the rest of the group is loud and talking. If no one notices and comments—either teacher or peers—then he will probably stop coming in quietly and start talking like the rest of the class. In this case his quiet, appropriate behavior has been _____ .

9. Extinction can be used effectively with which one of the following behaviors:

___ a. attempted strangling of peers.
___ b. asking irrelevant questions.
___ c. femininity in male student.
___ d. swearing and coarse language.

7. reinforce (or reward)

8. extinction;
   extinguished

9. b

10. Which reasons explain why extinction would not be effective with the other three behaviors in 9:

  ____ a. difficult to remove reinforcers.
  ____ b. not operant behavior.
  ____ c. possible acceleration of behavior unwise.
  ____ d. a and c above.

11. When a child complains about an assignment or activity, we generally try to argue the merits of the program. Unfortunately, when the complaining occurs frequently, it can be a habit or a way of getting attention and the discussions only further the child's complaining. _____ can be an effective method of reducing negative behaviors and complaining.

10. d

11. Ignoring
    (Extinction)

SET 3: Time Out (TO)

For some behaviors, simply ignoring the child is not enough to curtail the behavior without excessive expenditure of time. For these behaviors, Time Out from positive reinforcement represents an effective alternative (see Walker, Mattson, and Buckley, 1969; Bijou, Birnbrauer, Kidder, and Tague, 1967).

The method of Time Out removes the child from a situation in which he can receive reinforcement. This differs from extinction in that the method of extinction removes the reinforcing stimulus rather than the child.

Generally this method utilizes a Time Out room (sometimes called a "quiet room"). The child is requested to go to the Time Out room for a period of time (usually ten minutes). The room is devoid of interesting objects so that during this period he talks to no one, has nothing to play with, and has no academic assignment. If ready to begin work after that time, he may return to the classroom. It is important that the teacher not lecture or scold the child or let her expression show she is upset. Often getting a teacher upset is reinforcing to a child and is "worth" suffering aversive consequences.

The potential misuse of Time Out is great enough that it should be used only if other techniques prove unsuccessful. Recommendations arising from its use in public schools include the following:

A.   Discuss the rationale for its use fully with the principal, parents, and students. It is desirable to have signatures of parents indicating they have discussed the technique with school personnel and agree with the concept.

B.   If the Time-Out room is an enclosed area, make sure it meets with local fire codes. For this reason, as well as for effective management, the door should open easily from the inside (preferably without a doorknob) and should *never* have a lock or external restraint. If the child attempts to leave before his time is up, his timer is just reset. The room should be large enough for a desk and chair, have overhead lighting and adequate ventilation, and not be frightening.

C.   Always keep a list of the occurrences when the child is sent to the room, the time, and the reason. It should not be necessary to use the quiet room more than one or two times per week for any person in the entire class.

D.   The child should never be sent to the Time-Out room for longer than five minutes for grades K-2, or ten minutes for older children. If the child acts up while in the quiet room, it may be necessary to reset the timer for the same length of time—but never longer. This is *not* solitary confinement; it is a way to calmly de-fuse potentially danger-ous situations. The child should come out calmer and ready to begin work.

E.   Two children should not be placed in the quiet room together. They can be put in sequentially, or a tem-porary quiet area can be arranged for a second child.

F.   The teacher should be ready to accept the child back into the classroom. The child has accepted the conse-quences for her behavior and, therefore, is abiding by class-room rules.

12. To be effective, there must be no desirable stimuli for the child when placed in Time Out. Check any of the following statements which would be a way to use Time Out.

_____ a. placing a child in a room with only a chair and blank walls.
_____ b. placing a child in the hallway.
_____ c. placing the child in the front corner of the class-room, as an example to the rest of the class.
_____ d. sending a child to the principal's office to do odd jobs.

12.   a   (all others may give chance for reinforcement)

13. When is it best to lecture the child on why he shouldn't break rules?

_____ a. before putting him in Time Out so the misbehavior is fresh in the child's mind.

_____ b. after Time Out to serve as a reminder of how to behave.

_____ c. never. The rule is restated and the child is put in Time Out with no additional comment.

13. c

14. Not all classrooms need or should consider using the Time-Out concept. It could be considered under the following circumstances:

_____ a. a child gets along well in all classes except one where he seems to have a "personality clash" with the teacher.

_____ b. a large number of children are exhibiting extreme behavior problems.

_____ c. one or two children show violent behavior with the teacher or other students.

14. b, c

SET 4: Reinforcing Incompatible Behaviors
        (Counterconditioning)

Incompatible behaviors are behaviors which are difficult to perform simultaneously with the deviant behavior. When these behaviors are being performed, they do not allow for maladaptive behaviors to occur. This procedure is illustrated by the frequent technique of giving a lost, crying child an ice-cream cone. The child cannot cry and enjoy the ice-cream cone at the same time.

Reinforcing incompatible behaviors is a useful tool for eliminating undesirable behaviors and building up desirable behaviors. It increases the effectiveness of other reinforcement or punishment techniques when used in conjunction with them. Thus it will be doubly effective if we reinforce in-seat behavior at the same time that we punish out-of-seat behavior.

In some cases where it is difficult to work with the deviant behavior, working with an incompatible behavior may be more profitable. The problem of truancy illustrates this. If we only punish the child for not coming to school, we may increase his dislike for school. Yet if reinforcers were used, it would seem unfair to reinforce him for just coming to school. A better alternative would be to make coming to school desirable. The teacher can determine what would make school desirable—less frustrating assignments (or conversely, more challenging assignments), changes in text, earned privileges, teacher attention, etc.—and make these available to the child.

EXHIBIT

The technique of reinforcing incompatible behaviors was used in a study of conditioning attending behavior (Walker and Buckley, 1968).

"Phillip was a bright (WISC: 116), underachieving male who, upon referral, exhibited a number of deviant behaviors that were incompatible with successful, task-oriented performance in the classroom setting. Phillip

59

was enrolled in the fourth grade and his chronological age at referral was 9—6. His deviant behaviors in the classroom reportedly included verbally and physically provoking other children, not completing tasks, making loud noises and comments, coercing attention from the teacher, talking out of turn, and being easily distracted from a given task by ordinary classroom stimuli such as minor noises, movements of others, changes in lighting conditions, and a number of other stimuli common to a classroom setting. A series of observations from the regular classroom . . . indicated he attended to assignments only forty-two percent of the time."

During treatment phase "the subject was told that when a given interval of time had elapsed, in which no distractions had occurred, a click would sound and the experimenter would enter a single check mark in a cumulative recording form which would indicate that the subject had earned a point. The subject was told that attending to the click represented a distraction and would result in loss of the point for that interval. The subject was allowed to exchange his points for a model of his choice at the conclusion of the treatment period.

"Systematic manipulation of the reinforcement contingency during the individual conditioning program produced significant changes in the response measures of percentage of attending behavior and frequency and duration of nonattending behavioral events. Upon withdrawal of the reinforcement contingency, the behavior returned to pretreatment levels, thus indicating that the alteration in behavior was due to the manipulated, experimental variable rather than to the influence of an unknown or chance variable."

Once the behaviors were under experimental control, procedures were established for programming generalization and maintenance of the behavior outside the experimental setting. (pp. 245-250)

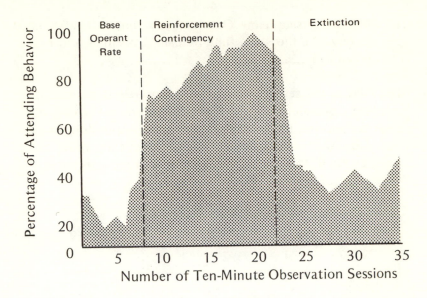

Figure 2. Percentage of attending behavior in successive time samples during the individual conditioning program.

15. Examples of incompatible behaviors in class are:

    a.   distractive behavior and (talking/working on task).
    b.   whispering to peer and (responding to teacher/out-of-seat).
    c.   reading a comic book and (singing/leaning back in chair).

16. For a child who has a high rate of nonattending, distractive behavior, reinforcement for _____ should reduce the number of distractions.

15. a. working on task
    b. responding to teacher
    c. singing

16. working on task (or attending to task)

61

17. Mr. T is using Time Out for each time Bill talks back rudely. At the same time he can give smiles and praise when Bill _____ .

18. Mrs. S has several students who shout out answers during discussion. She is trying to eliminate "talking out" by ignoring those children and only responding to children with raised hands. She will get even more rapid results if, when a child remembers to raise his hand, she _____ him.

17. responds properly (or isn't rude)

18. praises (or reinforces)

SET 5:   Stimulus Satiation

Satiation is the method of presenting a reinforcing stimulus at such a high rate that it is no longer desirable and may be aversive. Having a child write a dirty word which he has used 500 times is an example of the technique of satiation. What was desirable to say once becomes undesirable after repeating it 500 times.

Due to the differences in satiation level, both among children and among reinforcers, it is difficult to determine the effectiveness of this technique. In some cases it effectively curtails the behavior, and in others the effects are only short term. When physiological reinforcers, novel reinforcers, or conditioned reinforcers are involved, it is difficult to use satiation.

The process of satiation, however, should be kept in mind, particularly since desirable behaviors are sometimes inadvertently diminished through satiation of a reinforcer (Landau and Gewirtz, 1967).

EXHIBIT

Teodoro Ayllon (1966) used the procedure of stimulus satiation with a female mental patient. The patient had a nine-year history of towel collecting and storing when they were made available to her. It was reported that about twice a week the nurses simply removed the towels from the patient's room.

At the beginning of the experiment the nurses stopped removing the towels. Instead they gave towels to the patient without comment intermittently throughout the day. The number of towels given her per day was increased from 7 the first week to an average of 60 per day by the third week.

The author reports, "During the first few weeks of satiation, the patient was observed patting her cheeks with a few towels, apparently enjoying them." By the fourth and fifth weeks the patient exhibited comments

such as, "Get these dirty towels out of here." After the
total towels in the room reached 625, the patient began
voluntarily removing them. This continued until she had
almost no towels and maintained for the next 12 months
at 1.5 towels per week.

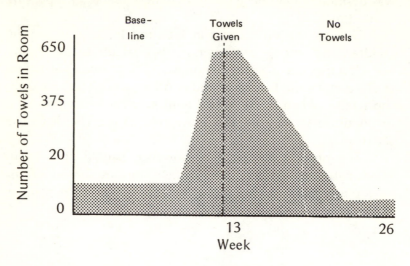

Figure 3. "A response, towel hoarding, is eliminated when
the patient is given towels in excess . . . ." (Ayllon,
1966)

19. A child who tips back in his chair is frequently annoying
to teachers. One method of eliminating the behavior is
by satiation. If the child is told to lean back in his chair
all day and to come down under no circumstances except leaving the room, we can expect the behavior of
leaning back to (increase/decrease) according to the
theory of _____ .

19. decrease;
satiation

64

20. If a child *is required* to practice on the piano for great lengths of time each day, what once was fun (reinforcing) may become _____ through satiation.

21. If satiation of a reinforcer is taking place, the child's behavior which obtains the reinforcer will (increase/decrease).

22. If a grade school child is required to perform the behaviors listed below for an extended period of time, which three of the behaviors could we expect to no longer be reinforcing:

_____ a. TV watching.
_____ b. pencil sharpening.
_____ c. standing to work.
_____ d. eating food.
_____ e. crawling on floor.
_____ f. stealing money.

20. aversive

21. decrease

22. b, c, e

SET 6: (Simple) Stimulus Change

Certain responses seem to occur only when specific environmental conditions are present. Thus, by altering the conditions we can eliminate the behavior.

Stimulus change is simply the process of changing the environmental contingencies to reduce the chances of the behavior occurring.

The technique of stimulus change is very common in the regular classroom. If a child continually pokes at the student next to him, the teacher generally moves his desk away. By moving the desk the teacher is changing the stimulus that brought about the poking.

Stimulus change has the short-term effect of terminating undesirable behavior. Yet if the stimulus conditions are returned to the original state (the child's desk is moved back) there is a chance the maladaptive behavior will *reappear*.

23. When a child giggles and talks in the back of the line while going to gym class or the lunch room, by placing him at the front of the line the teacher usually stops the giggling and talking. This is an example of _____ change. The stimulus in this case is (proximity to friends and distance from teacher/giggling and talking).

24. For a child who sucks his thumb, gloves can be placed on his hands to prevent the *response* of _____ _____ .

25. Adaptive school behaviors can be affected by stimulus change as well as maladaptive behaviors. A well-known example is the child who knows his lines for the school play very well but forgets them in front of the audience. The change in stimuli, in this case _____ _____ , produced a change in the child's behavior (response).

26. Whenever possible, it is desirable to have quiet and noisy activities in separate areas of the room. Thus, sitting at desks can be a signal for quiet individual work, and sitting in a circle on the floor can be a signal for active discussion. When used in this manner, the teacher is managing behavior by changing the _____ rather than the consequence.

23. stimulus;
    proximity to friends and
    distance from teacher

24. thumb sucking

25. audience size

26. stimulus

27. Name the six techniques mentioned for decreasing deviant behavior.

1. _____   4. _____
2. _____   5. _____
3. _____   6. _____

27.   (see Summary, page 69)

SUMMARY

In this section a variety of techniques for decreasing or eliminating deviant behavior were discussed. They include:

1. Punishment—physical and/or verbal reprimand by a social agent.
2. Extinction—withholding the reinforcement for the behavior.
3. Reinforcing behaviors incompatible with maladaptive behavior.
4. Time Out—removing the child from the reinforcing climate.
5. Satiation—presenting a desirable stimulus at such a high rate that it loses its reinforcing value and may become aversive.
6. Stimulus change—altering the environment so that the eliciting stimulus is no longer present.

The technique a teacher chooses for any one behavior will depend on the seriousness of the misbehavior, how often it occurs, and practical matters such as length of time needed, adaptability to classroom, and reaction of parents, peers, and students.

Chapter 4 Measuring Behavior

SET 1: Which Behaviors to Measure

Before we can ask *why* a child is behaving as he is, we need to ask *what* he is doing and *how often* the behavior occurs.

In observing a child, it is important not to imply motives or feelings from the behaviors. It is only guessing to say a child "looks guilty," "hates his teacher," "is lazy," "is hyperactive," etc. The maladaptive behaviors a child exhibits should be described in terms of events that can be easily counted and recorded.

Not only should implying motives and feelings be avoided, but also trying to find original causes. After looking at the behavior, we can assume why it occurs, but we must be willing to change that assumption when we get feedback from our recordings or raw data.

Once the behavior has been described as something that can be observed and recorded, it is necessary to specify the dimensions of the behavioral category. The category should be defined so that any time the child exhibits a given behavior the teacher can easily say the behavior does or does not fall within the category. Some classroom behaviors such as talking out, not completing assignments, and tardiness can be easily defined. Behaviors such as sloppy writing, smart talk, silly behavior, and nonattending are more difficult to define.

The criterion for the category may vary with the behavior, the setting, and the child. What may be defined as noisy in the classroom would be considered "normal" on the playground.

In a research study (Walker and Buckley, 1968), the following observable behaviors were classified as nonattending events: "(a) looking away from the text and answer sheet by eye movements or head turning; (b) bringing an object into his field of vision with head and eyes directed toward paper (other than pencil, book, and answer sheet necessary for the task); and (c) making marks other than those necessary for the task (doodling)." (p. 246)

1. Before recording behaviors, they must be stated in concrete or _____ terms and the limits of the category specified.

2. "The child enters the room following the final bell to begin class" describes (lazy habits/tardiness).

3. Which of the following are concrete observations:

____ a. he is frustrated by math.
____ b. he throws incomplete math papers in the wastebasket.
____ c. he has an inferiority complex.
____ d. he comments that no one likes him.
____ e. he frequently stands on the sidelines during physical education.
____ f. he is lazy.

1. observable

2. tardiness

3. b, d, e

4. Dan disrupts the classroom frequently by banging his desk. His teacher decides to count the number of occurrences. His behavior could best be counted by recording:

____ a. attention getting events.
____ b. hostility.
____ c. banging on desk.
____ d. insecure behavior.

5. "Noise: Whenever the student is talking loudly, yelling, or making other deliberate inappropriate noises—such as banging books or scraping chair back and forth—which is actually or potentially disruptive to others."* This description of noisy behavior (could/could not) be used effectively to record such behaviors.

*Code category from observation form developed by R. S. Ray, D. A. Shaw and G. R. Patterson, Oregon Research Institute, 1968.

4. c

5. could

SET 2: Recording How Often Behaviors Occur

Not only is it important to describe behaviors in observable terms, it is also important to tell how often the behavior occurs.

The statement "He throws incomplete math papers into the wastebasket" becomes more precise when changed to "He threw four incomplete out of ten assigned math papers into the wastebasket in the last two weeks."

Scientists have found that our own estimations of how often a behavior occurs are extremely inaccurate when compared with actual recordings. For example, an extremely annoying behavior may seem to occur more frequently than it actually does.

It is useful in dealing with some behaviors to record the same behavior of a classroom peer. What may seem like a high rate of "silly" behavior by a first grader may be a rather typical response exhibited by his peers as well. If he is not producing the behavior at a higher rate, yet it is still *more* annoying, we need to look at other variables.

The level at which a response normally occurs before we intervene is called the operant level. The period of recording this operant level is called the baseline period.

Because our own estimations are inaccurate, taking baseline recordings before we start to change behaviors is essential to determining the success of our technique.

After several days of taking baseline recordings, the teacher is ready to begin his treatment procedure. Recordings should be continued during treatment. If the intervention technique is later stopped, the recording should continue at infrequent intervals as a check on maintenance of good performance in the child (follow-up recordings).

6. Recordings taken before starting to change a child's behavior are called _____ recordings.

7. Baseline recordings are essential to knowing the
_____ of intervention.

6. baseline

7. results (success)

8. Recordings can be divided into three phases in relation to treating, or intervening in, a problem. These three phases are:

a.

b.

c.

8. a. baseline (pre-, before)
   b. treatment phase (interven-
      tion phase, during)
   c. follow-up (post phase, after)

SET 3:   How to Record Behaviors

Behavior recording, when efficient, requires very little time. There are a variety of efficient methods for recording behaviors. The common element in all of them is consistency. The small amount of time expended in getting accurate and consistent recordings will be paid for by improvement in the child's behavior.

Probably the easiest way to record behaviors is to simply tally the behavior each time it occurs. The only prerequisite for keeping such tallies is that the behavior be clearly defined in observable terms so that you know what to include.

Continuous recording of each behavioral event (*frequency count*) is best used for behaviors that are discrete units occurring less than twenty times a day. (Discrete is used to describe units of behavior that are easily defined as separate and distinct.)

Other recording techniques must be used for behaviors that occur at extremely high rates, are difficult to continuously observe, or cannot be broken down into small, discrete units.

A technique called *time sampling* can be used to record behaviors that occur at high rates, or are difficult to observe over time. Time sampling involves recording behavior at certain times during the day rather than continuously. This method will give an accurate count of behaviors when extended over long periods of time.

In using the time sampling technique, predetermined times should be set up to observe the behavior. The length of each recording period depends on the specific behavior. Accurate recordings could be made by recording the first five minutes of each hour, fifteen minute blocks three times a day, or one-half hour each day.

When the time period over which the behavior occurs varies from day to day, a useful technique for recording is to compute the *rate* at which the behavior occurs. Rate is computed by dividing the number of behaviors by the length of time the behavior is recorded.

For behaviors which occur for long periods of time and which are hard to break into discrete units, the *duration* of the behavior can be recorded. The duration is the period of time during which each separate instance of the behavior occurs.

Thus the length of each behavior might be recorded for behaviors such as "in-seat behavior," independent reading, or transition between subject areas.

9. Recording behavior only at specified time intervals during the day is called time sampling technique, as opposed to _____ recording of each response.

10. Observing the child only once a day for fifteen minutes is also an example of the time _____ technique.

11. Time sampling is useful with behaviors difficult for a classroom teacher to record continuously all day, such as:

____ a. nonattending.
____ b. muscle tics.
____ c. eye-blinking.
____ d. nail-biting.
____ e. babbling.
____ f. all of the above.

12. If a teacher looks at the child every hour—9:00, 10:00, etc.—and notes whether the behavior is present or absent, she (is/is not) using the time sampling technique.

9. continuous   11. f

10. sampling   12. is

13. A teacher observes a child for ten minutes, and the behavior she wants to change (accelerate or decelerate)
occurs four times during that period. To obtain the rate
per minute, she divides 4 by 10. The behavior occurred
_____ times per minute.

14. A child completes 17 arithmetic problems in 8 minutes.
His production rate is _____ problems per minute.

15. If a child gets out of his chair frequently and moves
around the room, we can record the number of times
out-of-seat (frequency recording) or the amount of time
in-seat, which is a way of recording _____ .

13. .40

14. 2.1

15. duration

SET 4: Interpreting Recordings

The recording aspect of behavioral alteration cannot be over-emphasized. There are many techniques available which effect changes in behavior. It is possible, even with the use of a "good" technique, not to effect the desired change or even accelerate maladaptive behavior. Without data, the treatment program cannot be critically evaluated and altered.

Transferring the raw data to graphs facilitates "reading" the data. Two easily used graphs are the bar graph (frequency histogram) and the line graph (frequency polygon). A line graph is generally used because of the ease of making and reading one. The vertical and horizontal axes should be clearly labeled as to the behavior recorded. It is a matter of practice that the vertical axis represents the behavior being counted and the horizontal axis the number of observation periods.

The placement of observations from all three phases (baseline, treatment and follow-up) on the same graph facilitates comparison. These three phases can be separated by vertical dotted lines on the frequency polygon.

16. During one week a behavior is observed to occur 5, 8, 12, 15, and 14 times. Plot the points on the bar graph below.

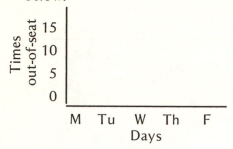

Observations

17. A classroom teacher has recorded number of times out-of-seat each day for one child. Label the axes for her recordings:

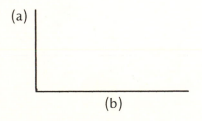

a. _____   b. _____

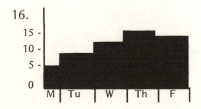

17. a. number of times out-of-seat
    b. number of observations (days)

81

18. The child was out of his seat 10 times the first day, 13 the second and 8 the third. Plot the data points on the frequency polygon below:

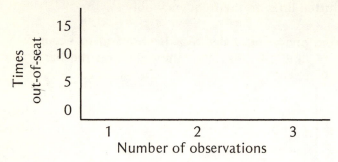

18.

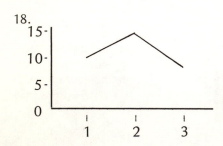

19. Mr. N is recording the number of arithmetic problems correct for each child. He is also interested in the amount of time required to finish the problems each day. Therefore, he is going to use rate (in this case number of correct problems per minute). His data for Phillip show:

Number Correct	Time to Complete
15	2 min.
7	1 min.
18	4 min.

Plot the three data points on the graph below:

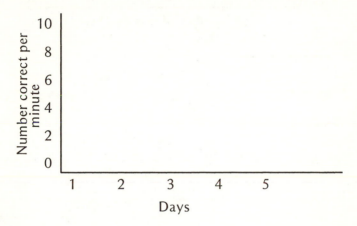

19.

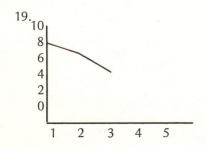

20. In the graph below the teacher has divided the data with a dotted vertical line each time she began a new phase. Assuming the data are complete, label the three phases.

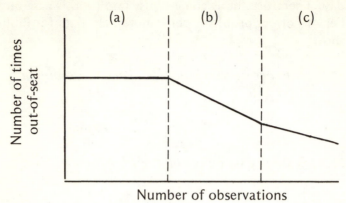

a. _____

b. _____

c. _____

21. Based on the graph in 20, did the teacher's treatment procedure reduce out-of-seat behavior? (yes/no)

20. a. baseline
    b. treatment
    c. follow-up

21. yes

22. Assume that you are trying to increase the number of problems correct out of 10 for a child. The graph from your recording looks as follows:

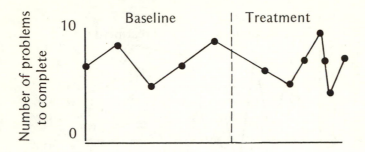

From the basis of the data, should you continue the procedure? (yes/no) Explain.

22. no. No change occurring. One should not continue unless there is some reason to believe the program had not been in effect long enough to get change.

23. Miss V has a child who sings or hums to himself and disturbs the children around him. She decided to use *extinction* and told the children to ignore him when he is singing or humming. Her data thus far appear below. Should she continue the procedure? (yes/no)

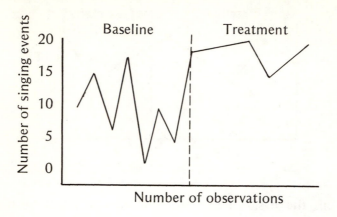

23. yes (see p. 51)

24. The following is a graph of fighting behavior for a fourth-grade boy.

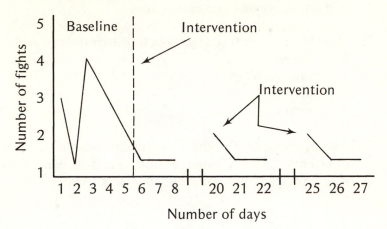

| | = omission of days (e.g., 9-19 omitted, 23-24 omitted)

From the data, which technique has been used?

___ a. extinction.
___ b. punishment.
___ c. token reinforcement.

24. b. Cues: abrupt change with intervention; re-appearance of behavior over time

87

SUMMARY

1. It is important to record behavior in observable terms without implying motives or causes.

2. Methods of recording adaptable to classroom use are:
   a. frequency
   b. time sampling
   c. rate
   d. duration.

3. The behavior of the child should be recorded prior to intervention, during intervention, and following intervention (if the intervention technique is terminated).

EXHIBIT

The following study (Bijou, 1966) illustrates many of the procedures discussed in Part I.

"The subject, Ann, was above average intelligence and came from a family in the upper-middle socio-economic class. After 6 weeks in the nursery school, which is considered the normal period required for adaptation, it was noted that she spent a small part of her time with children. Most of her time was spent with adults or alone, sometimes in constructive occupations, other times just sitting and standing about. Most of her time with adults was devoted to trying to attract the teacher's attention with her collection of rocks, pieces of wood, etc., and talking about her scratches, bumps, and bruises. Her speech was hesitant and low, and at times she showed tic-like behaviors.

"Two trained observers recorded Ann's behaviors each morning under the regular and usual conditions of school attendance. With the exception of snack time, time spent with children and time spent with adults was recorded at 10-second intervals over 5 mornings. Data derived provided a baseline and information on the reliability of the raters. Over the 5-day period Ann spent about 10 percent of her time with children and about 40 percent with adults.

"On day 6, one of the teachers was assigned to go to Ann immediately and remain with her and her group as long as she was with children. Under these circumstances the teacher watched, commented favorably on Ann's play and especially the play activity of the group. The teacher was also instructed to give Ann minimal or no attention when she was alone or with adults, including the teacher herself. Under these conditions, which were in effect for 6 days (day 6 to day 11), Ann spent about 60 percent of the mornings in play with her peers and less than 20 percent in contact with adults.

"On day 12, and the 5 succeeding days, the contingencies were reversed, that is, the baseline conditions were again reinstated. During this period (day 12 to day 16) interactions with children fell to about 20 percent and interactions with adults rose to about 40 percent.

"On day 17, and during the succeeding 8 days, the teacher again reinforced Ann for contact and play with peers. Over this time span, play with children stabilized at about 60 percent, and contacts with adults at about 25 percent. Adult attention for interaction with children was gradually made more intermittent, and the schedule of nonreinforcement of adult contacts was gradually relaxed during the last days of this period.

"Six days (day 31) after the last day of the study (day 25) the first post-study check was made to see whether the changes persisted. Other checks were made on the thirteenth, fifteenth, and twenty-sixth days after completion of the main study. These data showed that the changes were maintained in that Ann was spending about 54 percent of her mornings with children and about 18 percent with adults." (pp. 63—64)

Part 2 Application

Chapter 5 Modifying Classroom Behavior

SET 1: The Classroom

Knowledge of environmental effects on behavior is equally important in the self-contained classroom and the open classroom. The important considerations are that the teacher is aware of the impact of the environment on behavior and is able to develop behavioral objectives as carefully as academic objectives. A teacher needs to be aware of behavioral excesses that impede performance as well as deficits that prevent a child from achieving maximum benefit from the classroom.

The specific intervention program required for modifying a classroom behavior will usually vary according to the behavior being modified and the child. However, there is a general set of procedures which can be followed in the process of modifying most classroom behaviors.

1. *Develop individual behavioral and academic goals for each child in the classroom.* In the past, teachers have generally set yearly academic goals for themselves, that is, subject areas to be covered during the year. While this approach provides structure for a teacher and accountability to the principal, of necessity it reduces options for the children. If the goal is to complete a given math book by the end of school, then some students may be moving at a pace slower than needed and many more may be moving at a more rapid pace than that which allows them to understand the material. When the goals and materials are individualized, each child is mastering the material as it is introduced. Once a child is succeeding in school and feels good about herself and her

place in school, many behavior problems will be reduced. For those that remain, the same individualized approach can be used for behavior as for academics. With behavioral goals in mind, the teacher may begin by setting goals of teaching James to sit in his seat for at least ten minutes at a time, fourteen complete papers a week from Mario, raising his hand in discussions for Fred, and reducing hitting of peers for Denise.

2. *Decide how often the behavior is currently occurring.* A child cannot begin a behavioral program without prior assessment any more than he can begin a reading program until the teacher has determined his reading level. To do so would be similar to handing a child a book to read without ever monitoring his reading skills.

Generally about a week of baseline behavioral data is needed. However, if the behavior is inconsistent or there is reason to believe other factors from home or school have interfered during that week, additional time may be needed.

3. *Set daily steps.* Not only should a target behavior (end goal) be set, but daily goals as well. The daily goal should be above what the child can do on the average, but equal to or below the highest level he can perform. Assume the goal is to help a child consistently score 80 percent or better. His present average is 30 percent. If his highest score has been 50 percent, then the daily goal should begin between 30 percent and 50 percent. To begin above 50 percent may mean the child cannot perform well enough to sample the reward; thus, it might not be effective.

4. *Involve the child.* With behavioral intervention techniques a child should be an active participant in changing his own behavior. To gain his cooperation he should feel a part of developing the behaviors expected, the goals and the rewards. The teacher should decide on the outside parameters before discussing the program with the child and then give him choices within those parameters. The child should be helped to feel that the teacher is an ally in the entire process. Thus, a success is a success for both teacher and child. Likewise, a failure is shared equally by teacher and child.

5. *Decide on the environmental change.* It is important to remember that this can be an agreed upon change before the behavior occurs or one that comes immediately following the behavior, or both. The problem with changing two things at once is the problem of knowing which changes are responsible for changing the behavior. This is an extremely important consideration for research but in the classroom the major problem may be that more program is used than is actually needed. At the same time, this shotgun effect is more likely to ensure instant success.

6. *Record the behavior.* Throughout the behavior change process the behavior should be recorded to determine success.

7. *Change the program.* If the program is not producing changed behavior, the data should be studied to discover the problem. Is the goal appropriate? Is the reinforcer effective? Has the child had an opportunity to sample the reinforcer? Is the behavior being monitored frequently?

Even an effective program needs change. The teacher should gradually increase the behaviors expected and may want to use a variety of reinforcers for increased interest. The authors have found that periodic bonuses or surprises add interest and cooperation with the program. Such things as occasional bonuses for getting certain random problems correct; a timer set for an unknown time which "catches" children sitting in their chairs or working on assignments and rewards them with three additional minutes of recess, etc.

A recurring concern among teachers and educators in the use of behavior modification procedures relates to the issue of fairness and the equitable treatment of all children. Teachers have expressed concern that if a deviant or disruptive child is treated in a special way, that is, he is rewarded, other children in the class will observe this and learn to "act out" in order to gain access to the reinforcement system. There is no empirical evidence that this occurs and the authors have not observed this phenomenon in any of their research and training activities. However, it does seem to be a logical concern and one that is well within the realm of possibility in most regular classroom settings.

The desirability of providing children with prosthetic devices to help them see or hear better is generally agreed upon. Some children need glasses to read or a seat in the classroom near the blackboard to see the print. The child with behavior problems also needs prosthetic devices such as tokens, charts, etc., to help him perform at his maximum. If this is explained to the other children and teachers in this manner, the extra "tools" are generally accepted without difficulty. Beyond an explanation, there are a number of possible alternatives to this concern.

A strictly private arrangement can be established between the teacher and child where the child's daily performance is covertly rated by the teacher. If an agreed upon reinforcement criterion is achieved, then the child earns a special privilege at home. A reinforcement procedure of this type can be both highly effective and unobtrusive.

This problem can also be dealt with through the use of group contingencies. For example, if there are one or more behavior problem children in a teacher's classroom, a group contingency can be developed for the entire class wherein the class is treated as a single child. A set of classroom rules governing appropriate behavior can be developed and the class rewarded whenever *all* children are following the rules. With this contingency, one hopes that the behavioral level of the entire class as well as of the individual behavior problem children would be responsive to the group contingency. Since no individual children are singled out and treated in a special way using a group contingency, it is possible that such a contingency would not be either sufficiently direct or powerful to control the behavior of individual children who are moderately to severely deviant in the classroom.

A third alternative is to set up an individual contingency for a behavior problem child at school, but have only group activity rewards earned which are then shared equally with peers. In this contingency arrangement, the individual child is singled out and known to peers; however, the earned rewards are made available on an equal basis to all children. Thus, children are much less likely to act out in order to be treated in a special way with such a contingency. In fact, research has shown that a child's peers can be extremely supportive of his efforts to achieve the reward criterion in such situations (Walker and Buckley, 1972).

Of the three alternatives discussed, the third is the most desirable and the second the least desirable when dealing with a deviant behavior pattern presented by an individual child. It is possible, of course, to add a special individual privilege at home to the activity earned at school in the third alternative, thus potentially increasing its effectiveness still further.

1. If a child is given an individualized approach in his academic work and begins to find success in school, often his behavioral problems are _____ .

2. The first step in classroom management is:

  ____ a. develop a list of classroom rules.
  ____ b. decide on behavioral goals.
  ____ c. let the children know who is boss.

3. The baseline level must be established next. The behavior is observed in order to get an estimate of its rate or _____ .

4. Teachers have expressed concern that normal children will learn to "_____ _____" in order to gain access to a reinforcement system being applied to an individual behavior problem child.

5. The available evidence on this question (does/does not) support such a view.

1. reduced   4. "act out"

2. b   5. does not

3. frequency

6. Which of the following is *not* an appropriate response to this concern:

___ a. set up a private contingency between the child, teacher, and parents.
___ b. use a group contingency in the hope that it will control the behavior of individual behavior problem children as well.
___ c. convince teachers that the issue is not serious and probably will not affect the behavior of other children in the class.
___ d. set up an individual contingency wherein group activity rewards are earned that are shared equally with classmates.

7. There is a possibility that a group contingency would not be powerful enough to have an impact upon the behavior of individual behavior problem children. (true/false)

6. c   7. true

SET 2:   Increasing Coping Skills in the Classroom

While the acting out, disruptive child poses a serious management problem for the teacher, children who are extremely withdrawn, or those who have severe academic deficits, present an even more rigorous challenge to the teacher's skill. These children are not behavior problems in the traditional sense, but their lack of social and academic skills can seriously handicap their classroom performance. When learning theory principles are used to build up or condition behaviors which are extremely weak, we speak of a prosthetic application since the treatment goal is to remediate a deficit in some area of functioning. Methods of strengthening a behavior include the use of differential reinforcement, social reinforcement, token reinforcement, and the Premack hypothesis. The following series of frames provides examples of how these techniques can be used in the classroom.

8. In prosthetic applications of learning theory, extensive use is made of the Premack hypothesis which states that high probability behaviors can be used to reinforce and thereby _____ low probability behaviors.

9. If running, jumping, and yelling are high probability behaviors for five-year-old kindergarten boys, and sitting still, working quietly, and paying attention are low probability behaviors, then these high probability behaviors can be programmed to _____ and strengthen the low probability behaviors.

10. We could require, for example, that the boys produce twenty minutes of sitting still, working quietly, and paying attention in exchange for two minutes of running, jumping, and yelling in the gym. In this way, the _____ probability behaviors are being used to strengthen the _____ probability behaviors.

11. As another example, suppose that a child detests reading—low probability—and is very interested and skilled in science—high probability. How could you use the Premack hypothesis most effectively?

____ a. require equal amounts of time spent in reading and working on science projects.
____ b. require small amounts of reading in exchange for large amounts of time spent in science.
____ c. require moderate to large amounts of reading in exchange for small amounts of time spent in science activities.

8. strengthen

9. reinforce

10. high;
    low

11. c

12. In conditioning very weak responses, it is necessary to _____ the learning situation so that competing or interfering responses are controlled.

13. It would be difficult to teach listening skills to a child in a chaotic and uncontrolled classroom setting. Before we could teach listening skills, we would have to gain _____ of the learning situation.

14. For learning to be effective, we have to eliminate conditions which suppress or _____ the desired behavior from occurring. One way of doing this is to structure the learning situation so there is a high probability that the desired response will be emitted and rewarded.

15. There are three types of positive _____ which the teacher can program and control in the classroom setting. These include: (1) nutrient, (2) abstract, and (3) social reinforcers. Nutrient reinforcers usually consist of candy or food. Abstract reinforcers include points, tokens, gold stars, or grades. Social reinforcers refer to expressions or gestures of praise, attention, interest, approval, and affection.

16. Most classroom behavior can be controlled and regulated without the use of nutrient reinforcers. (true/false)

12. arrange (program, structure, or set up)

13. control

14. prevent (preclude)

15. consequences (or reinforcers)

16. true

17. There are many (extrinsic/intrinsic) reinforcers which operate naturally in the classroom environment to reinforce and maintain academic responses. These intrinsic reinforcers include mastery of a task, acquisition of new or interesting knowledge, task completion, positive feedback associated with making correct responses, etc. It would be very (easy/difficult) for the teacher to manipulate such intrinsic reinforcers directly.

18. There are a small number of children in the school setting who do not have the necessary skills to produce such _____ reinforcement for themselves. There are others who are not motivated to seek such reinforcement. There are also students for whom task mastery, task completion, and acquisition of new knowledge are simply not reinforcing. These children are often referred to as underachievers who have either learning or behavioral disorders. Such children usually require some form of _____ , positive reinforcement to build or to strengthen the required academic and social behaviors which contribute to success in school.

19. It is important to remember that all "problem" children do not respond to the same reinforcer(s). One child may prefer to work for small amounts of free time to engage in some favorite activity such as reading, art work, or science. With another child, systematic teacher attention and praise may be sufficient to maintain his attempts at appropriate classroom behavior. With still another, it may be necessary to reinforce with tokens which can be exchanged for a model or toy. For an intervention program to be effective, the _____ must be appropriate for the child.

17. intrinsic;   18. intrinsic;   19. reinforcer
    difficult   external (or extrinsic)

103

20. The child's classroom behavior should be brought under the eventual control of _____ reinforcers, dispensed by his learning environment (teachers, peers, materials).

21. Social reinforcers, dispensed by the teacher, are occasionally neutral or even aversive stimuli for some children because of a long history of negative connotations associated with their dispensement—scolding, scowling, verbal abuse, warnings, frowns, etc. In these instances, the incentive value of teacher-dispensed social reinforcers can be enhanced systematically by pairing _____ social reinforcers with points, stars, or tokens which can be exchanged for back-up reinforcers such as free time, grades, or special privileges.

22. As much as possible the regular classroom teacher should use rewards that are available within the classroom or cost little or no money. Which of the following rewards meet those criteria:

____ a. a good note home.
____ b. special additional work projects.
____ c. charting progress.
____ d. contingent recess.
____ e. extra time for certain academic subjects.
____ f. models to build.

20. social (intrinsic, or natural)

21. positive

22. a, b, c, d, e

23. If a child is capable of doing the assignments but frequently fails to complete them, which technique could be used:

    _____ a. calling his name each time you see him not working.

    _____ b. setting a goal with the child for when he can complete the work and then setting a timer as a visual reminder.

    _____ c. send his incomplete papers home at night.

24. If a child does not enjoy a certain assignment, he can be told that if he obtains a certain percentage correct that he will not have to do the last five problems. This is an example of _____ reinforcement, which can also be used to bring about behavior change.

23. b

24. negative

SET 3: Reducing Maladaptive Classroom Behavior

Children in the classroom produce behaviors which are at high strength and which are also highly variable in both form and rate. These behaviors can be classified along such dimensions as overt/covert, high rate/low rate, and appropriate/inappropriate for purposes of analysis and description. The teacher is usually most concerned with those child behaviors that are at high rates, which are of an overt nature, and are inappropriate to successful classroom performance. Often large amounts of time and energy are spent attempting to control these behaviors. This management problem is further complicated by the fact that these behaviors are of such high strength that the teacher's control over them is usually only temporary. Examples of such behavior include general hyperactivity, talking out, short attention span, disturbing others, daydreaming, temper tantrums, wandering around the room, etc. The teacher's goal is not to completely eradicate these behaviors from the child's repertoire, but to reduce their rates to manageable proportions within the classroom setting.

The behaviors described above are nonproductive in the classroom setting since they disrupt the instructional process and actively compete with successful academic performance. The goal of effective classroom management is to weaken or suppress these competing behaviors in order to facilitate the learning process. In behavior technology, there are a number of techniques which can be used to reduce the frequency of inappropriate classroom behavior including extinction, subtracting points or privileges (cost), Time Out, stimulus change, and counterconditioning.

25. A number of classroom behaviors such as tapping pencils, not working, daydreaming, disturbing others, talking out, etc., are classified as teacher irritants. These behaviors are often maintained by the _____ which they elicit from the teacher.

26. If a teacher scolds, frowns at, or warns a child each time he talks out, she may be (weakening/strengthening) the very behavior she is trying to (weaken/strengthen).

25. attention (response, or reinforcers)

26. strengthening; weaken

27. If the teacher suspects that her attention is maintaining talking out, she could test this assumption by systematically _____ her attention from the behavior.

28. If talking out showed a sudden increase following withdrawal of attention and then a gradual decline in rate, the teacher would have established a (functional/nonfunctional) relationship between adult attention and talking out.

29. In some conditioning programs, the individual can earn positive reinforcers for producing appropriate behavior and can *lose* a portion of his earned reinforcers for producing _____ behavior.

30. Response cost or cost contingency is a form of punishment where earned _____ are subtracted upon the production of deviant behavior.

27. withholding (or varying)

28. functional

29. inappropriate

30. reinforcers (or tokens)

31. Sometimes a child has shown he knows the material but does not do well on a formal test. How could the environment be changed to help reduce his test anxiety?

____ a. present the material in a manner he feels most comfortable with initially, for example, handwritten, orally, on a chalkboard, etc.

____ b. practice the material frequently to a level of overlearning.

____ c. begin the child with very easy items and gradually increase the difficulty.

____ d. present the material in a manner which will initially help form a set—all addition together, phonetically consistent words—until the child feels comfortable with tests.

____ e. all of the above.

32. A well-established procedure for transfer between classes generally reduces the amount of misbehavior occurring. This is an example of changing the environment (before/after) the behavior to make it less likely that the misbehavior will occur.

33. A noisy classroom can be quieted by a variety of unobtrusive signals. Which of the following could be used unobtrusively in the classroom as a signal that the class is too noisy.

____ a. lowering or turning out the lights.

____ b. shouting above the noise for the class to be quiet.

____ c. a red "stop" circle placed at the front of the room.

____ d. stopping talking until the children are attending.

____ e. sounding a chord on the piano.

31. e. All of the above   32. before   33. a, c, d, e

109

SET 4: Procedure for Shaping a Behavior

As mentioned earlier in Chapter 1, shaping refers to a process in which a new response is built into the behavioral repertoire through the reinforcement of successive approximations to some terminal performance. The skill to be acquired is described in functional terms and broken down into components which are conditioned by gradually raising the criterion for reinforcement. Shaping is especially useful in the acquisition of complex skills which are not readily acquired through demonstration, trial and error, or rote learning.

34. Select the behavior or skill which is to be _____ and break it down into small, discrete units which can be arranged in a sequence.

35. Provide a learning situation in which competing responses are controlled and the probability (increased/decreased) that the desired response will be emitted. Structure the situation carefully, monitor the performance continuously, and provide positive feedback *and* cues for correct responses.

36. Select a _____ to which the child is responsive.

37. Shape each discrete unit of the behavior separately and in the proper _____ . Reinforce successive _____ to the final performance of each component in the sequence. Raise the criterion for reinforcement gradually. Make the reinforcement (immediate/delayed) and continuous for appropriate responses.

34. acquired (learned)	36. reinforcer (reward, or consequating event)
35. increased	37. sequence; approximations; immediate

38. When all components in the sequence have been
    _____ , link them together through a process called
    chaining. Only reinforce production of the complete re-
    sponse from this point on.

39. Gradually shift from a continuous to an _____
    schedule of reinforcement and fade out the tangible
    reinforcement.

40. Monitor the behavior as necessary and keep
    _____ on the number of times it is performed to
    criterion as determined by rate, frequency, or percent-
    age correct.

38. mastered (achieved, or
     completed)

39. intermittent

40. records (data, or charts)

SET 5:   The Generalization and Maintenance
of Change in Child Behavior

In producing change in behavior the hope is for permanent changes which will be utilized in all settings. Unfortunately, there is a tendency of human behavior not to generalize across settings. The research literature in psychology and education provides overwhelming evidence that behaviors tend to be situationally specific (Herman and Tramontana, 1971; O'Leary and Drabman, 1971; Wahler, 1969, 1975). That is, human behavior in large part appears to be a function of the situation in which it occurs and is highly responsive to the stimuli, setting events, and controlling variables that exist within such situations. To the extent that there is a close "match" of these variables across settings, behavioral consistency within and across them can be expected.

Given that child behavior is situation specific, one would then not logically expect behavior changes produced in one setting, through alteration of existing contingencies in that setting, to generalize to nontreatment settings in which deviant behavior has occurred at equivalent or even higher levels. With a few exceptions (Hauserman, Walen, and Behling, 1973; Kazdin, 1973; Walker, Mattson, and Buckley, 1971) this is precisely what the research literature is showing (Herman and Tramontana, 1971; O'Leary and Drabman, 1971; Wahler, 1969, 1975; Walker, Hops, and Johnson, 1975).

This is a particular problem in situations where psychological/educational treatments are administered within artificial or special settings and generalization of changed behavior to natural settings is expected. Treatments administered within the psychologist's office or clinic and within special or resource classrooms have been very popular in the last two to three decades. However, the effectiveness of such treatment in impacting upon behavior in natural settings, where treatment procedures are not implemented, is being increasingly questioned by psychologists and educators (Stuart, 1972; Tramontana, 1971).

Tramontana (1971) suggests that even if such generalization effects were in evidence, one must wonder about the effects the unmodified natural environment would eventually have on the changed behavior. Under such circumstances, it would be expected that the deviant behavior would be restrengthened and that the experimentally produced behavior changes would eventually extinguish. The limited data base on this question seems to support Tramontana's research (Herman and Tramontana, 1971; O'Leary and O'Leary, 1976; Walker and Buckley, 1972, 1974).

The available evidence suggests that effective generalization and maintenance of changed behavior does not automatically occur when treatment procedures are abruptly withdrawn (Birnbrauer, Wolf, Kidder, and Tague, 1965; Walker, Mattson, and Buckley, 1971). Unless systematic fading procedures are used (O'Leary, Becker, Evans, and Saudargas, 1969) or attempts are made to transfer behavioral control to readily available reinforcers such as teacher praise (Greenwood, Hops, Delquadri, and Guild, 1974) or efforts are made to reprogram the environment in which maintenance is expected (Patterson, McNeal, Hawkins, and Phelps, 1967; Walker and Buckley, 1972; Walker, Hops, and Johnson, 1975), it is unlikely that the changed behavior will maintain automatically.

41. The goal of behavior change procedures has been to produce comprehensive and _____ changes in human behavior.

42. Human behavior appears to be, in large part, a function of the _____ in which it occurs and is highly responsive to the stimuli, setting events, and controlling variables that exist within such situations.

43. To the extent that there is a close "_____" of these variables across settings, behavioral consistency within and across them can be expected.

44. Given that child behavior is situation specific, one (would/would not) logically expect behavior changes produced in one setting to generalize to nontreatment settings in which deviant behavior had occurred at equivalent or even higher levels.

45. The available evidence shows that, with few exceptions, effective generalization and maintenance of changed behavior (does/does not) automatically occur when treatment procedures are abruptly withdrawn.

41. enduring
    (lasting)

42. situation

43. "match"

44. would not

45. does not

114

46. Treatments administered within the psychologist's office or clinic, or within special classrooms, have a (low/high) probability of producing behavior changes in natural settings such as the regular classroom, playground, or home where such changes are expected.

47. Even if such generalization effects were achieved within a special setting, it is (likely/unlikely) that they would persist within the unmodified natural environment.

48. Which of the following would *not* be appropriate techniques for facilitating the achievement of generalization and maintenance effects:

_____ a. gradually fading out the use of tangible or abstract reinforcers.

_____ b. transferring control of changed child behavior to natural reinforcers such as praise and positive feedback.

_____ c. motivating peers to reinforce and support the child's changed behavior.

_____ d. asking the child why he can't seem to learn to control his behavior like other children do.

_____ e. providing random, noncontingent free time activities to the child in the posttreatment maintenance period.

_____ f. giving the child feedback on a daily basis regarding the generalization and maintenance of his changed behavior and occasionally rewarding him for doing well.

46. low

47. unlikely

48. d, e

Clues Concerning the Generalization
and Maintenance of Child Behavior

The following suggestions are designed to assist the reader in dealing with the difficult and complex problems presented by the general failure to achieve generalization and maintenance of changed child behavior.

1. As a rule, do not expect changed child behavior to generalize from treatment to nontreatment settings (from school to home or vice versa). If you wish change(s) to occur in such settings, extend the contingency or treatment procedures to them.

2. The extent to which you can expect maintenance of gains following withdrawal of formal treatment procedures is highly variable. In most cases, you should not expect maintenance to occur indefinitely without implementing procedures specifically designed to achieve it. Such techniques would include: (a) extensively applying teacher praise to support and "build in" the changed behavior; (b) providing occasional and unexpected group activity rewards to the child and the whole class when he has done well in maintaining the changed behavior; (c) giving the child frequent feedback, at least daily, as to how he is doing in maintaining the changed behavior; (d) teaching the child to monitor his own behavior as a maintenance strategy and reinforcing him for *accurate* counts of his own behavior; (e) using systematic and gradual fading procedures to slowly remove any treatment procedure. An abrupt termination of treatment procedures almost invariably produces a return to pretreatment levels of behavior.

3. In attempting to extend contingencies to other settings, such as from the regular classroom to the playground, to hallways, to the lunchroom and to the home, it is extremely important to involve social agents (principal, parents, monitors, aides, etc.) within these settings in the actual direct implementation of the contingency procedures. The contingency procedures should be implemented in *exactly* the

116

same fashion in all these settings so that a consistent pattern of child behavior will be produced. In order to achieve this goal, all these social agents will need to be carefully trained and monitored in the correct application of the procedures.

4.   Plan to program a modified form of the treatment procedures for an indefinite period of time in order to insure the long-term maintenance of changed child behavior within whatever settings treatment was implemented and maintenance is expected.

SET 6: Involving Parents
in School-Based Intervention Programs

Increasingly, parents have been involved in the implementation of school programs designed to change child behavior. Parent involvement has ranged from the simple dispensing of school-earned rewards at home (Ayllon, Garber, and Pison, 1975; McKenzie, Clark, Wolf, Kothera, and Benson, 1968), to teaching parents of the target child to apply differential reinforcement procedures at home (Martin, Burkholder, Rosenthal, Tharp, and Thorne, 1968), to involving parents directly in efforts to produce changes in the child's behavior at home that may facilitate appropriate school behavior (Johnson and Katz, 1973).

Parent involvement has a number of potential therapeutic advantages. For example, parents may be more supportive of and cooperative with a school treatment program in which they are involved. Second, the program can establish a positive dialogue between parents and the school concerning the child's school performance. It is possible that such a dialogue would build in a measure of consistency in child behavior across home and school settings. Third, it seems likely that the more social agents there are involved in the treatment program, the more likely it is that a significant impact will be achieved on the child's overall behavior pattern and that the behavior will generalize across agents. Finally, it may be that parent involvement actually produces changes in the child's home behavior.

Parents in general and particularly parents of deviant or disruptive children are a valuable resource for teachers and other school personnel in managing child behavior. It is indeed unfortunate that, in the past, parents of problem children and school personnel have tended to blame each other for disruptive child behavior in the classroom. School personnel often feel that parents have not taught their child an appropriate behavior pattern, acceptable to the school, and that the root causes of the child's school behavior problems stem from this lack of training. Conversely, parents often charge that educators are not doing their job in educating children generally and that the child's school behavior is the educators' responsibility. This polarization of attitudes has reduced the opportunities for parents and school personnel to work together cooperatively in developing positive responses to child behavior problems at school.

Research has indicated (Johnson and Katz, 1973) that parents are competent in the following areas: (a) praising child success at school; (b) making individual rewards available at home that have been earned at school; and (c) using contingency procedures to change child behavior at home. Parents require some initial training and monitoring over time in order to acquire competence in each of these areas. However, once their skills are developed, their participation can be an extremely valuable addition to school intervention programs.

The authors and others have used a combination of group activity rewards earned and delivered at school, and individual rewards earned at school but delivered at home, to effectively change child behavior (Hops, Beickel, and Walker, 1975). Anecdotally, it was noted that some children prefer home rewards only, others school rewards only, and some both home and school rewards equally. Whenever possible, it is desirable to program both home and school rewards for appropriate child behavior at school in order to provide the most powerful set of conditions for motivating children to change their behavior.

49. There has been a general (increase/decrease) in the involvement of parents in school-based intervention programs designed to change child behavior.

49. increase

50. Parent involvement in the process of changing child behavior has included a number of options, including which of the following:

_____ a. dispensing school-earned rewards at home.

_____ b. applying differential reinforcement procedures at home.

_____ c. using role playing techniques to get children to "act out" their anxieties and frustrations.

_____ d. using home tutoring and other change procedures to facilitate changes in child behavior at school.

51. In the past, parents and schools have tended to _____ each other for a child's behavior problems at school.

52. Researchers have usually found parents to be quite competent in which of the following areas:

_____ a. praising child success at home.

_____ b. developing insights into the true meaning of child behavior.

_____ c. delivering school-earned rewards at home.

_____ d. applying contingencies to change child behavior at home.

53. Parents usually require some initial _____ and monitoring over time in order to acquire competence in each of the above skill areas.

54. Programming a combination of school and home rewards for child behavior at school is probably (superior/inferior) to providing only school or home rewards.

50. a, b, d   52. a, c, d   54. superior

51. blame   53. training

120

55. An added advantage of providing home rewards is that some teachers do not mind having children earn rewards at school but _____ to their being delivered and consumed at school.

55. object

References

Ayllon, T. Intensive treatment of psychotic behaviour by stimulus satiation and food reinforcement. In Ullman, L. P. and Krasner, L. (Eds.) *Case studies in behavior modification.* New York: Holt, Rinehart and Winston, 1966.

Ayllon, T., Garber, S., and Pison, K. The limitation of discipline problems through a combined school-home motivational system. *Behavior Therapy,* 1975, *6,* 616-626.

Bandura, A., Ross, D., and Ross, S. A. Transmission of aggression through imitation of aggressive models. *Journal of Abnormal Social Psychology,* 1961, *63,* 575-582.

Bandura, A., Ross, D., and Ross, S. A. Imitation of film-mediated aggressive models. *Journal of Abnormal Social Psychology,* 1963, *66,* 3-11.

Bandura, A. and Walters, R. H. *Social learning and personality development.* New York: Holt, Rinehart and Winston, 1963.

Becker, W. C., Madsen, C. H., Jr., Arnold, C. R., and Thomas, D. R. The contingent use of teacher attention and praise in reducing classroom behavior problems. *Journal of Special Education,* 1967, *1,* 287-307.

Bijou, S. W. Experimental studies of child behavior, normal and deviant. In Krasner, L. and Ullman, L. P. (Eds.) *Research in behaviour modification.* New York: Holt, Rinehart and Winston, 1966.

Bijou, S. W., Birnbrauer, J. S., Kidder, J. D., and Tague, C. Programmed instruction as an approach to teaching of reading, writing and arithmetic to retarded children. In S. W. Bijou and D. M. Baer (Eds.) *Child development: Readings in experimental analysis.* New York: Appleton-Century-Crofts, 1967.

Birnbrauer, J. S., Wolf, M. M., Kidder, J., and Tague, C. E. Classroom behavior of retarded pupils with token reinforcement. *Journal of Experimental Child Psychology*, 1965, *2*, 219-235.

Estes, K. W. An experimental study of punishment. *Psychological Monographs*, 1944, *57*(263), 40.

Gaasholt, M. University of Oregon, Personal communication, 1969.

Greenwood, C. R., Hops, H., Delqaudri, J., and Guild, J. Group contingencies for group consequences in classroom management: A further analysis. *Journal of Applied Behavior Analysis*, 1974, *7*, 413-425.

Hall, R. V., Lund, D., and Jackson, D. Effects of teacher attention on study behavior. *Journal of Applied Behavior Analysis*, 1968, *1*, 1-12.

Hauserman, N., Walen, S. R.; and Behling, M. Reinforced racial integration in the first grade: A study in generalization. *Journal of Applied Behavior Analysis*, 1973, *6*, 193-200.

Herman, S. H. and Tramontana, J. Instructions and group versus individual reinforcement in modifying disruptive group behavior. *Journal of Applied Behavior Analysis*, 1971, *4*, 113-119.

Hops, H., Beickel, S., and Walker, H. M. *Contingencies for learning academic and social skills (CLASS): Manual for consultants.* Eugene, OR: Center at Oregon for Research in the Behavioral Education of the Handicapped, University of Oregon, 1975.

Johnson, C. A. and Katz, R. C. Using parents as change agents for their children: A review. *Journal of Child Psychology and Psychiatry*, 1973, *14*, 181-200.

Johnston, J. M. Punishment of human behavior. *American Psychologist*, 1972, *27*(11), 1033-1054.

Kazdin, A. E. The effect of vicarious reinforcement on attentive behavior in the classroom. *Journal of Applied Behavior Analysis*, 1973, *6*, 71-78.

Kuypers, D. S., Becker, W. C., and O'Leary, K. D. How to make a token economy fail. *Exceptional Children*, 1968, *35*(2), 101-109.

Landau, R. and Gewirtz, J. L. Differential satiation for a social reinforcing stimulus as a determinant of its efficacy in conditioning.

Journal of Experimental Child Psychology, 1967, *5*, 391-405.

Martin, M., Buckholder, R., Rosenthal, R. L., Tharp, R. G., and Thorne, G. L. Programming behavior change and reintegration into school milieu of extreme adolescent deviates. *Behaviour Research and Therapy*, 1968, *6*, 371-383.

McKenzie, H. S., Clark, M., Wolf, M. M., Kothera, R., and Benson, C. Behavior modification of children with learning disabilities using grades as tokens and allowances as back-up reinforcers. *Exceptional Children*, 1968, *34*, 745-752.

Mechner, F. A notation system for the description of behavioral procedures. *Journal of the Experimental Analysis of Behavior*, 1959, *2*, 133-150.

O'Leary, K. D., Becker, W. C., Evans, M. B., and Saudargas, R. A. A token reinforcement program in a public school: A replication and systematic analysis. *Journal of Applied Behavior Analysis*, 1969, *2*, 3-13.

O'Leary, K. D. and Drabman, R. Token reinforcement programs in the classroom: A review. *Psychological Bulletin*, 1971, *75*, 379-398.

O'Leary, K. D. and O'Leary, S. G. Behavior modification in the school. In H. Leitenberg (Ed.) *Handbook of Behavior Modification and Therapy*. Englewood Cliffs, NJ: Prentice-Hall, 1976.

Parke, R. D. Effectiveness of punishment as an interaction of intensity, timing, agent nurturance, and cognitive structuring. *Child Development*, 1969, *40*, 213-235.

Patterson, G. R., McNeal, S., Hawkins, N., and Phelps, R. Reprogramming the social environment. *Journal of Child Psychology and Psychiatry*, 1967, *8*, 181-195.

Piaget, J. *The child's conception of the world.* New York: Harcourt, Brace and World, 1929.

Skinner, B. F. *The technology of teaching.* New York: Appleton-Century-Crofts, 1968.

Stuart, R. B. Behavior modification techniques for the educational technologist. In R. C. Sarri and F. F. Maples (Eds.) *The Schools in the Community*. Washington, DC: National Association of Social Workers, 1972.

Thomas, D. R., Becker, W. C., and Armstrong, M. Production and elimination of disruptive classroom behavior by systematically varying teacher's behavior. *Journal of Applied Behavior Analysis*, 1968, *1*, 35-45.

Tramontana, J. A review of research on behavior modification in the home and school. *Educational Technology*, 1971, 61-63.

Wahler, R. G. Setting generality: Some specific and general effects of child behavior therapy. *Journal of Applied Behavior Analysis*, 1969, *2*, 239-246.

Wahler, R. G. Some structural aspects of deviant child behavior. *Journal of Applied Behavior Analysis*, 1975, *8*, 27-42.

Walker, H. M. and Buckley, N. K. The use of positive reinforcement in conditioning attending behavior. *Journal of Applied Behavior Analysis*, 1968, *1*, 245-250.

Walker, H. M. and Buckley, N. K. Programming generalization and maintenance of treatment effects across time and across settings. *Journal of Applied Behavior Analysis*, 1972, *5*, 209-224.

Walker, H. M. and Buckley, N. K. *Token reinforcement techniques*. Eugene, OR: E-B Press, 1974.

Walker, H. M., Hops, H., and Johnson, S. M. Generalization and maintenance of classroom treatment effects. *Behavior Therapy*, 1975, *6*, 188-200.

Walker, H. M., Mattson, R. H., and Buckley, N. K. Special class placement as a treatment alternative for deviant behavior in children. In F. A. M. Benson (Ed.) *Modifying deviant social behaviors in various classroom settings*. Eugene, OR: Department of Special Education Monograph #1, University of Oregon, 1969.

Walker, H. M., Mattson, R. H., and Buckley, N. K. The functional analysis of behavior within an experimental classroom setting. In W. C. Becker (Ed.) *An empirical basis for change in education*. Chicago: Science Research Association, 1971.

Winett, R. A. and Winkler, R. C. Current behavior modification in the classroom: be still, be quiet, be docile. *Journal of Applied Behavior Analysis*, 1972, *5*, 499-504.

Wolf, M., Risley, T., and Mees, H. Application of operant conditioning procedures to the behaviour problems of an autistic child. *Behaviour Research and Therapy*, 1964, *1*, 305-312.

Zimmerman, E. H. and Zimmerman, J. The alteration of behavior in a special classroom situation. In Ulrich, R., Stachnik, T., and Mabry, J. (Eds.) *Control of Human Behavior.* Glenview, IL: Scott, Foresman, 1966.

Suggested Readings

1. Benson, F. A. M. (Ed.) *Modifying deviant social behaviors in various classroom settings.* Department of Special Education, University of Oregon, 1969, No. 1.

2. Homme, L., Csanyi, A., Gonzales, M. and Rechs, J. *How to use contingency contracting in the classroom.* Champaign, IL: Research Press Co., 1968.

3. Millenson, J. R. *Principles of behavioral analysis.* New York: Macmillan, 1968.

4. Patterson, G. R. *Living with children: New methods for parents and teachers.* Champaign, IL: Research Press Co., Revised, 1976.

5. Skinner, B. F. *The technology of teaching.* New York: Appleton-Century-Crofts, 1968.

6. Walker, H. M. and Buckley, N. K. *Token reinforcement techniques.* Eugene, OR: E-B Press, 1974.

ABOUT THE AUTHOR

Nancy K. Buckley is Director of Child and Adolescent Services at Spanish Peaks Mental Health Center in Pueblo, Colorado. Mrs. Buckley completed her graduate work at the University of Oregon. Following graduation, she served as the research psychologist for the Engineered Learning Project at the University of Oregon. She has published *Token Reinforcement Techniques* with Dr. Hill M. Walker as well as numerous chapters, monographs, and articles. She is currently on the Editorial Boards of *Journal of Applied Behavior Analysis* and *Child Behavior Therapy*. Her research interests include application of social learning principles in the classroom, the home, and with behaviorally disordered youths. Mrs. Buckley has directed classrooms and residential facilities for emotionally disturbed youth.

ABOUT THE AUTHOR
Hill M. Walker received his Ph.D. in Special Education at the University of Oregon in 1967 and is currently Professor of Special Education at the University of Oregon. Since 1971 he has directed CORBEH, a federally funded research and development center whose goal is the development and validation of behavior management packages for specific behavior disorders. From 1966 to 1970, Dr. Walker co-directed the Engineered Learning Project (ELP) with Nancy Buckley. ELP was a federally funded research project designed to produce cost effective identification and treatment procedures for primary grade children experiencing behavior problems in the classroom setting. Dr. Walker's major research interests are in the areas of screening/identification, behavior management, and the generalization and maintenance of treatment gains. He has published several books and numerous articles in these areas and is the author of the Walker Problem Behavior Identification Checklist.